SCOTTISH PRIDE

SCOTTISH PRIDE

101 Reasons to be Proud of Your Scottish Heritage

Heather Duncan

CITADEL PRESS
Kensington Publishing Corp.
www.kensingtonbooks.com

CITADEL PRESS BOOKS are published by

Kensington Publishing Corp.
850 Third Avenue
New York, NY 10022

All Kensington titles, imprints, and distributed lines are available at special quantity discounts for bulk purchases for sales promotions, premiums, fund-raising, educational, or institutional use. Special book excerpts or customized printings can also be created to fit specific needs. For details, write or phone the office of the Kensington special sales manager: Kensington Publishing Corp., 850 Third Avenue, New York, NY 10022, attn: Special Sales Department; phone 1-800-221-2647.

First printing: March 2004

10 9 8 7 6 5 4 3 2 1

Printed in the United States of America

Library of Congress Control Number: 2003108997

ISBN 0-8065-2552-5

Contents

Introduction

My son, who is only one-quarter Scottish, says that all you need to know about Scotland you can learn from *Braveheart.* I hate to contradict him, but although the 1996 film gave an important boost to the Scottish tourist industry, most of its scenes were shot in Ireland.

Scotland covers only half the amount of land as England does, about 30,500 square miles. However, roughly 80 percent of the British coastline is in Scotland.The Scottish population accounts for approximately over 9 percent of the population of Britain, while in London Scots account for around 12 percent. There are now about 25 million people of Scottish lineage living abroad, compared with only 5 million in Scotland itself. Scotland has 790 islands, of which only 130 are inhabited.

Considering its size, Scotland and its history have had an amazing impact on the world. To a warrior nation fighting for its independence throughout the centuries, the names of William Wallace, Robert the Bruce, and Rob Roy are heroes whose lives are portrayed in legends, chronicles, novels, and films. It was a Scot who discovered penicillin, changing the way the world treated disease. Television, the telephone, and the Macintosh raincoat were all invented by Scots. The work of

Robert Burns, Scotland's greatest poet, is read in schools all over the world.

Scotland had an enormous influence in the founding and growth of America. Woodrow Wilson, a United States president with Scottish ancestry, said, "Every line of strength in American history is a line colored with Scottish blood."

Many Scottish groups and societies throughout Canada and America have taken the anniversary of the Declaration of Arbroath (1320) as the date to celebrate their Scottish roots. We Scots have so much to be proud of: great writers, historians, artists, beautiful countryside, scientists, and inventors—and don't forget that we produce and supply whisky to the whole world!

PART I:

CULTURE AND HISTORY

1

Actors

Did you know that the world's most sophisticated British undercover agent was actually Scottish? Sean Connery, perhaps best known as James Bond, was born in Scotland in 1930. Connery was cast as British agent James Bond in *Dr. No* in 1962 over many more famous actors, although Ian Fleming—the creator of the fictional British agent 007—was quoted as saying "He is not exactly what I envisioned." The role of James Bond made Sean Connery a major star of the 1960s. He has since moved on, playing starring roles in *The Untouchables,* for which he won an Oscar, and *The Hunt for Red October.* He also appeared in the popular fantasy film, *Highlander,* in 1986, this time as a Spaniard. Voted *People Magazine*'s "Sexiest Man Alive" in 1989, he is still swooning material as a senior citizen—not to mention an accomplished amateur golfer.

Although he was Scottish, David Niven was regarded by many film-

goers as the archetypal Englishman. Born in Kirriemuir in 1901, he served in the Highland Light Infantry. Niven resigned his commission and moved to the United States, where he began his acting career as an extra in 1935. He quickly gained a reputation as a suave and debonair gentleman through roles in *The Charge of the Light Brigade* (1936), *The Dawn Patrol* (1938), and *Raffles* (1940). Niven rejoined the British Army at the start of World War II, becoming a lieutenant colonel in the commandos. He agreed to act in two propaganda films during the war, and was honored by President Eisenhower on his return to Hollywood. Niven resumed his Hollywood career after the war, taking roles in almost 100 films, including many popular comedies. His later films include *Around the World in 80 Days* (1956); *Separate Tables* (1958), for which he won an Academy Award; *The Guns of Navarone* (1961); *The Pink Panther* (1964); and *The Sea Wolves* (1980).

Perceived as the quintessential English beauty, Deborah Kerr, born in 1921, was in fact a native of Helensburgh, Scotland. She led a successful career in British movies before moving to Hollywood. She is best remembered for her roles as the sizzling adulteress in *From Here to Eternity* (1953), as Anna the governess in *The King and I* (1956), and playing opposite Cary Grant in *An Affair to Remember* (1957), and also starred in such films as *Black Narcissus* (1946), *The Hucksters* (1947), and *The Prisoner of Zenda* (1952). In 1993 she was presented with an honorary Academy Award for Lifetime Achievement.

Despite having acted in more than four hundred Hollywood films, Donald Crisp was Scotland's great forgotten actor. Born in 1880 in Aberfeldy, he emigrated to the United States in 1906. His films included *Birth of a Nation* (1915), *Intolerance* (1916), *Dawn Patrol* (1938) with David Niven, *How Green Is My Valley* (1941), for which he was awarded an Oscar for Best Supporting Actor, and *National Velvet* (1944) with Elizabeth Taylor. Crisp, who died in 1974, was also an accomplished director and film financier.

Born Mary Gilmour in Glasgow in 1882, Mary Gordon traveled to America with a touring theater company. She went on to take character roles in more than two hundred Hollywood films between 1925 and 1950. She is perhaps best remembered for her screen portrayal of Mrs. Hudson, the housekeeper to Sherlock Holmes, a role she played nine times.

David Keith McCallum, born in Glasgow in 1933, made more than seventy films but is best remembered by most people as the Russian agent Ilya Kuryakin in the TV series *The Man from U.N.C.L.E.*, for which he was nominated for a Golden Globe award in 1966. He performed the spy role in various spin-off films, but was also successful in war films such as *The Long and the Short and the Tall* (1960), *The Great Escape* (1963), and *Mosquito Squadron* (1969).

Stage and film actor Tom Conti, born in 1941, was trained to be a classical pianist at Glasgow's Royal Scottish Academy of Music, but soon turned to acting as a career. Conti starred in *Reuben, Reuben* (1983), for

which he received an Academy Award nomination; *Heavenly Pursuits* (1986); and *Shirley Valentine* (1989).

Born in Perthshire and trained at the Royal Scottish Academy of Music and Dance in Glasgow, Alan Cumming became internationally known for his stage role in *Cabaret* as the Master of Ceremonies, which won him a Tony award. His film roles include work on the Bond film *Goldeneye* (1995) with fellow Scot Robbie Coltrane, *Circle of Friends* (1995), *Emma* (1996), and *SpiceWorld* (1997). In Scotland, he is best known for his TV role in *The High Life*.

Robert Carlyle was born in 1961 in Glasgow. He was inspired to take up acting after reading an Arthur Miller play. His films include *Trainspotting* (1996), *The Full Monty* (1997), *Angela's Ashes* (1999), and *The Beach* (2000). He was noted an OBE in 1999.

Ewan McGregor was born in 1971 and brought up in Crieff, a small, traditional country town. Leaving there to study acting in Perth and then in London, he first gained attention in the black comedy *Shallow Grave* (1994), then burst into the spotlight with the lead in *Trainspotting* (1996). The role of Obi-Wan Kenobi in the *Star Wars* prequels has kept him in the public eye.

Tom Fleming has had a long and illustrious career in radio, television, and the theater. His professional dramatic debut was in a company led and directed by Edith Evans in 1945. In 1952, he played the leading part in the first Scottish full-length drama production, *The Black*

Eye. In 1953, he cofounded the Edinburgh Gateway Company, and was a leading member of the Royal Shakespeare Company from 1962 to 1964. In 1965 he founded and became first director of the Royal Lyceum Company of Edinburgh. He served as director of the Scottish Theatre Company from 1982 to 1987.

Fleming has given many memorable performances on television, from Robert Burns and William Wallace to Jesus of Nazareth (the first time the part had been performed in front of television cameras) and Henry IV (earning him a nomination for Best Television Actor). Fleming is famous for his commentaries on royal and state occasions, including Queen Elizabeth's Coronation, her Silver Jubilee, two Royal weddings, ten funerals, and the enthronement of two Popes and three Archbishops. He was awarded an OBE in 1980 for services to the arts in Scotland.

2

Artists

With such a beautiful countryside and rich culture, it is no surprise that Scotland boasts many world-class artists.

Artist Allan Ramsay studied under the famous painter William Hogarth in London. He then traveled through Europe on his way to Rome, and that trip influenced his work. Returning to Edinburgh in 1738, he painted portraits and enjoyed Edinburgh society, where his friends included David Hume and Adam Smith. In London he painted portraits of royalty, and was so much in demand that he employed other artists such as Alexander Nasmyth to assist him. He is often referred to as the "Scottish Hogarth."

Sir Henry Raeburn, an Edinburgh painter born in 1756, is best known for his portraits of most of the society figures of his day, including Sir Walter Scott and David Hume. The University of Edinburgh has a major collection of his works.

William McTaggart, born in Aros in Kintyre (now Highland) in 1835, spent his childhood on the western coast of Scotland. Although he studied portrait painting in Edinburgh, he was best known for his Scottish landscapes. His most famous painting, "Through Wind and Rain," painted in 1875, shows the Scottish coastline, its harsh and cold weather, and the obvious struggle that sailors had in such windswept waters. The painting is in Dundee's art museum.

William McGregor McDonald Muir's paintings focus particularly on the local topography. His studies focus on the Girvan Harbour, its fishing boats and lifeboats, and the Girvan townscape against the backdrop of the Carrick Hills. In the summer of 1999, a William Muir painting dated 1882, "Sunset and Arran Hills from the Ayrshire Coast," was among the Ayrshire contributions to the festival exhibition "Scotland's Art" in the City Art Centre at Edinburgh.

Sir John Steell, born in Aberdeen, was Queen Victoria's sculptor in Scotland, and created many of the public statues in Edinburgh, including the bronze equestrian statue of the Duke of Wellington outside Register House, and the statue of Sir Walter Scott at the center of the Scott Monument.

Scotland is proud of its many architects. Robert Adam was an eighteenth-century architect noted for his elegant terraces in the New Town of Edinburgh, along with many other fine public buildings. He also contributed to the Georgian development in London.

David Bryce, born in 1803, was a proponent of the "Scottish Baronial" style of architecture. Examples of his work include Fettes College and the (new) Royal Infirmary in Edinburgh, as well as more than one hundred country houses.

Sir (Robert) Rowand Anderson, born in Edinburgh in 1834, was Scotland's leading architect around the turn of the twentieth century. He worked in many styles, from "Scottish Gothic" to classical, and his public buildings include the Scottish National Portrait Gallery, the McEwan Graduation Hall, and the medical school for the University of Edinburgh. Sir Basil Spence was born in India, but was educated and spent most of his working life in Edinburgh. He began his career in association with Rowand Anderson, and his work ranged from housing to commercial and public buildings. Coventry Cathedral is perhaps his most notable building.

James Stirling was born in Glasgow in 1926. From 1945 to 1950, he was trained in the Beaux Arts tradition at Liverpool University. He worked with Lyons, Israel & Ellis in London for several years before forming a partnership with James Gowan. Stirling and Gowan produced several influential buildings, starting a trend toward brick and exposed concrete. Stirling's early designs, especially for Cambridge and Oxford, often emphasized concept over aesthetic and utilitarian needs. His later works appeared more formal due to the influence of post-modern classicism. Criticized for his habit of continually altering his

fundamental architectural principles, Stirling used an experimental design approach that showed little commitment to one particular style. He designed many controversial buildings.

Charles Rennie Mackintosh, born in 1868, will always hold top honors as Scotland's most influential architect and designer. The Glasgow designer's style was a unique blend of art nouveau and Scottish Celtic traditionalism. Like Frank Lloyd Wright, his interior and furniture designs are as important as his buildings and his work is exhibited throughout the world. His most famous building is the Glasgow School of Art, the design of which was copied by many of his contemporaries.

3

Bagpipes

You either love them or hate them. Long considered instruments of the "common people," bagpipes were played mainly outdoors. Very little was written about them because of their association with peasants and other people of low social status, such as shepherds and farmers—even gypsies. Although stories of their origin vary (there are even said to have been bagpipes in the ancient Near East), bagpipes are now strongly identified with Scotland, especially in the form of the Highland Bagpipe.

Bagpipes developed from ancient hornpipes, and evolved into instruments with bag and drones in early European history, emerging as a familiar instrument by the twelfth century. The air pressure for the pipes comes from a bag of skin attached to them. (Today the bags are made of synthetic materials.) The pipes were being played in Scotland by the fourteenth century and in the Highlands by about the year 1400.

They achieved their current look in the late sixteenth and seventeenth centuries, at the same time that they overtook the harp as the musical instrument of Gaelic society and assumed a major role in Gaelic culture. They were played outdoors and in the great halls for dancing and entertainment.

Dynasties of pipers emerged, such as the MacCrimmons, MacKays, MacGregors, and Cummings, who performed the duties of official piper for their patrons through successive generations and sustained and generated the music of the bagpipe. The Highland bagpipe survived by virtue of the growth of empire and standing armies. Piping, both in Scotland and in Europe as a whole, has been characterized by a variety of music and playing styles.

When bagpipes arrived in America, they were not incorporated into bands or orchestras like other wind instruments. In fact, in 1899 a Chicago judge ruled that the bagpipes were not a musical instrument. Now a symbol of Scottish pride, they are played in parades, in Celtic festivals, and even at weddings. You will see them on St. Patrick's Day and the Fourth of July in parades, competitions, and Highland festivals.

A few years ago, we had a birthday party for our Glasgow-born friend, James Campbell, and hired a bagpiper to surprise and entertain the guests. Our most famous local Scotsman was greatly moved as the bagpiper played his way from the front of my house along the driveway to the backyard. The bagpipes were definitely the highlight of the party.

4

Birds and Other Wildlife

Scotland's moist terrain provides a perfect breeding ground for some very unusual birds and animals. Between 300 to 325 species of birds are recorded annually.

The largest bird is the golden eagle; its wingspan can reach up to six feet, but it can easily be mistaken for a buzzard. The eagle is now a protected species, so more of them should start appearing around Loch Lomond. The osprey has also received a similar new lease on life and is becoming more prevalent. It is a large bird with a white underside and large talons. It lives solely on fish, which it dives for—feet first—often becoming completely submerged. It is quite a sight to see the osprey explode from beneath the surface and fly off, carrying its catch torpedo-style. One bird common only to Scotland is the hooded crow. It is slightly larger than the normal crow and looks as though it is wearing a waistcoat.

At Loch Lomond, you can see mallards, swans, cormorants, and goosanders. One of the rarer sights is the black-throated diver. Loch Lomond also has lesser-spotted woodpeckers, siskens, fieldfares, and pied wagtails.

More than 150,000 seabirds return each year to the islands off the coast near North Berwick. The famous Bass Rock Island is the world's largest single rock gannetry and the mating ground for at least 40,000 pairs of gannets. The gannet is Britain's largest seabird, with a wingspan of nearly six feet. Although they are migratory and separated by thousands of miles at sea during the winter, gannets mate for life. They generally return to the same partner and the same nest each year. The first gannets usually return to Bass Rock in late January. They are spectacular fliers and dive at high speed into the sea with wings half closed in order to catch fish, hitting the water at speeds of over 60 miles per hour. They can live for over twenty years.

The fulmar resembles a gull at a distance, but up close its yellowish green bill can be seen to have distinctive tubular nostrils. In the course of digesting its meal, the fulmar produces a foul-smelling, sticky, oily substance that it can shoot for a distance of up to nine feet. Fulmars live at sea outside the breeding season and are graceful, spectacular fliers. The shag (also known as the green cormorant) is a close relative of the larger cormorant.

The kittiwake is a small gull, recognizable by its dipped-in-ink black

wingtips, distinctive "kittiwaking" call, and fast wing beats. It builds its nest on ledges and winters as far away as the coast of Greenland.

The razorbill is related to the extinct great auk. It winters in the Atlantic and Mediterranean and comes back to nest beginning in February. Both parents share the incubation period, but while the male spends his off-duty time at sea, the female sits close by her nesting mate.

The guillemot lives at sea outside the breeding season. It returns to land in autumn to jostle with its neighbors and stake its claim for a few inches of nesting space on a bare rock surface. It returns in April to lay a single pear-shaped egg, pointed at one end and broad at the other; if moved, it rolls in a tight circle, rather than falling into the sea.

Approximately 40 percent of the world's population of gray seals live around Britain, most of those in Scottish waters. Over three thousand gather around the Isle of May, making it Britain's largest eastern-coast breeding colony. The scientific name for gray seal means "sea pig with a hooked nose" and this "Roman nose" is even more accentuated in the males. The name gray seal is a bit of a misnomer, since there is a lot of variation in color from almost black bulls to creamy white cows to the luxurious silky white fur of newborn pups. In the seal world, there's no such thing as being "too fat" and in the cold North Sea waters, gray seals have six centimeters of blubber to keep them warm. Their cylindrical shape not only makes them streamlined for swimming, but also mini-

mizes heat loss. If they survive the dangers of being a pup, seals are relatively long-lived animals, often lasting longer than thirty years.

Atlantic gray seals can be seen all year round, but there are many more in October and November, when they give birth to their pups. The seals haul up at low tide at both ends of May Island, and can also be seen swimming at the base of the West Cliffs. Gray seals breed in winter, probably because when they evolved, the world was a colder and icier place. The fluffy white coat of the baby gray seal is a reminder of its snowy origins.

The best place to see Scotland's red deer is in the Loch Lomond area. Both males and females are red buff and stand about four feet at the shoulder. Although they can be seen year round, the best time to see them is in the latter part of the year, during the rutting season, when the stags are at their best, sporting a full set of antlers. Next largest is the fallow deer, which is about a foot smaller and stockier than the red. The males are dark reddish, while the young and the females have white spots on their flanks. The roe deer is the smallest native deer. Both male and female are a reddish brown with a white rump. They prefer the edges of fields and woods.

The Scottish wildcat or Highland tiger, although rarely seen, are still around. They are about twice the size of a domestic cat, with tabby markings and a long bushy tail. Another rare animal is the pine marten.

It is a member of the weasel family and is the size of a cat. You could easily mistake a weasel for a pine marten. There are otters too, but you have to be an early riser to catch a glimpse of them. Feral goats live on the steep sides of Loch Lomond, but sightings of these are rare. Foxes are also seen around the area, as is the indigenous red squirrel. These are mostly seen in the Highlands because the gray squirrel has driven them out of most of Great Britain. Many Scottish animals such as the red deer, rabbits, and hares depend significantly on heather for survival.

5

Brogues and Other Unfamiliar Languages

Many Scots understand Gaelic as well as most English people do. The Gaelic language is thousands of years old and at one time was the main language of Scotland. It is a beautiful language with its own tone and rhythm. Until the twelfth or thirteenth century Gaelic was spoken in all of Scotland.

The Celtic dialect called Scots Gaelic, or Erse, was heard in many parts of the Scottish Highlands, especially in the Hebrides. Throughout most of the rest of Scotland, however, a Scottish dialect of English has been spoken for almost as long as in England. This dialect, descended from the Northumbrian dialect of Old English, was first known as Inglis and then, during the eighteenth century, as Scots. Educated Scots during this period strove to speak and to write Scots or English with equal

fluency. Burns made his reputation writing Scots poetry, but he also wrote extensively using formal English diction. Boswell could easily fall into speaking Scots, but he worked diligently to eradicate "Scottisms" from his writing. Johnson was complimenting Boswell when he called him the "most unScottified" Scot he had ever met.

Today only about 66,000 people speak Gaelic, mainly in northwest Scotland and the Hebrides. Efforts are being made to halt its decline, and political and cultural societies are exerting pressure to reintroduce Gaelic in schools.

Although most Scots do not speak Gaelic, numerous Gaelic words and phrases linger in everyday speech and make it difficult for Americans and other foreigners to understand exactly what a Scot is saying. "Lose the rag" can mean to lose your temper. Mince, a finely chopped beef, is a popular dish in England and Scotland, but the word has also come to mean rubbish or nonsense as in, "He was talking a load of mince." Someone who is as "thick as mince" is extremely stupid. "Winch," which has ancient roots in the English "wench," for woman, is used to describe a romantic involvement with someone, as in "Are ye winchin?" When someone says they will see you "at the back of nine," they mean roughly 9:15. However, Scots do not say, in turn, "front of nine" to mean 8:45.

Most of Scotland's place names today can be traced to their Gaelic-

or Scottish-language roots, which include Loch for lake, Glen for valley, and Ben for hill. The longest single-word place name is Coignafeuinternich near Inverness. The shortest is I, the Gaelic name for Iona.

6.

Business Greats

The name of Andrew Carnegie, a native of Scotland, is well known in America, since he has left his name on a major university, a famous concert hall, and many libraries and other institutions. Then there was John Davison Rockefeller. He inherited Scottish blood from his mother and, in the nineteenth and twentieth centuries, with just $900, founded the Standard Oil Company, starting with a single refinery in Titusville, Pennsylvania. Many Scottish Americans became industrial giants, but Scotland itself was filled with many other great businessmen, whose businesses and fortunes stayed at home.

William Paterson, born in Tinwald, Dumfriesshire, in 1658, founded the Bank of England in 1694. He was also the main proponent of the Darien Farce, which established a Scottish trading colony in Central America. The colony was a disaster, and Paterson's wife and child died while there. He promoted the Union of the Parliaments, which was—at

least in part—driven by an attempt to make good his and Scotland's losses at Darien.

The eighteenth-century tobacco trade made fortunes for many of Glasgow's most prominent businessmen. During the boom decades of the 1760s and 1770s, tobacco lords enriched Glasgow. The industrial base of that city was boosted dramatically, and many of Glasgow's great streets and buildings were built from tobacco trade money. Albert Spiers, born in 1714, was one of Glasgow's most prominent tobacco lords. John Glassford, born in 1715, was second only to Spiers as a tobacco importer and was even more important as a ship owner. The handful of leading tobacco lords owned about twenty-five ships each. By 1775, Glasgow's tobacco merchants were at the height of their prosperity and were importing from Virginia, North Carolina, and Maryland more than half the tobacco brought into Britain. In 1771, four years before war broke out in America, the Clyde saw 46 million tons of tobacco imported into Glasgow. Of this, three million tons remained for British consumption while the remainder was exported to France and the Low Countries.

The names of the tobacco lords appear today as Glasgow street names: Ingram Street, Buchanan Street, Glassford Street, Virginia Street, Cochrane Street. Virginia Street was named after Virginia Mansion, the home of Spiers. Another prominent merchant, William Cunninghame, built an imposing mansion on Queen Street. This building was con-

verted into the Royal Exchange, became Stirling's Library, and is now the Gallery of Modern Art. America's victory in the War of Independence ended the golden era of tobacco. Many merchants suffered heavy losses and tobacco imports through Glasgow were diminished when direct trade began between the Americas and Continental Europe.

Textile was—and remains—a major industry in Scotland. The Coats family was famous for being one of the world's largest manufacturers. Industrialist Sir Peter Coats was born in Paisley in 1808. He founded a family business that became the leading textile thread manufacturer. His younger brother, Thomas, eventually became the driving force behind the company, pushing its expansion into the United States in the 1860s and 1870s. Thomas, who was noted for his philanthropy (he was said to have left more than a million pounds to charity), was knighted in 1869. Today the company retains its great stature.

Jute baron James Cox was born in Lochee, Dundee, in 1809. By 1827, Cox was running the textile business started by his father. He formed a partnership with his brothers in 1840 and built Cox Brothers into the largest jute-manufacturing concern in the world. By 1885 the company employed five thousand people. Cox invested in shipping and railways at home and in the United States, and eventually was made lord provost of Dundee between 1872 and 1875.

Industrial chemist Charles Tennant was born in 1768 in Ochiltree, East Ayrshire. After a weaving apprenticeship, Tennant set up a bleach-

field near Paisley. He became the foremost industrial chemist of his time, producing dyes and bleach for an expanding textile industry. Tennant made a fortune from a bleaching powder that he patented in 1799. His factory in North Glasgow became the largest chemical plant in the world at that time.

Tea, wine, and whisky were also major Scottish exports. Sir William Fettes, born in 1750, was a merchant and philanthropist who made his fortune from tea and wine. He left money to found Fettes College, a school dedicated to the education of poor and orphaned children; it is now one of Scotland's top private schools and still retains a tradition of scholarships for poorer children.

Brewer and philanthropist Dr. William McEwan, born in Alloa in 1827, set up his Fountain Brewery in Edinburgh in 1856. He later entered parliament and gave significant donations to Edinburgh and its university. His McEwan's Export beer is still popular today.

Even better known was Sir Thomas Lipton, grocer and entrepreneur, born in a tenement in Port Glasgow in 1850 to Irish parents. Lipton left school at ten and stowed away in a ship bound for America. Initially he worked as a farm laborer in Virginia and South Carolina, later working in a grocer's shop in New York. He must have absorbed American business flair, for five years later he was back in Glasgow opening what was to be the first shop in an extremely successful retail empire. Lipton revolutionized the retail grocery trade, developing many

marketing techniques that are still used by supermarkets today. He was particularly innovative in the tea business, selling different blends to different countries and using containers to help preserve freshness. It was Lipton who was the first to package tea in small, convenient tins to keep it fresh, preserve the flavor, and guarantee that customers received the correct amount of tea. By the turn of the century, tea was a popular beverage on both sides of the Atlantic. In ten years he was a millionaire, acquiring tea estates in Sri Lanka and meat processing factories in America. He summed up his business philosophy as, "Work hard, deal honestly, be enterprising, exercise careful judgement, and advertise freely but judiciously."

Lipton's source of relaxation was sailing, and he used his fortune to enter a succession of boats (all named "Shamrock") in the Americas Cup. In all he raced five times but never won. In 1910, he initiated soccer's World Cup. Lipton never forgot his native city, and upon his death he left a substantial amount of money to Glasgow and gave the city his extensive personal collection of newspaper clippings, photographs, and memorabilia.

Sir Alexander Grant, the son of a railway guard, was born in Forres in 1864. Grant began working in an office, but then became apprenticed to a local baker. He moved to Edinburgh, gaining employment with Robert McVitie. Here he found his niche, and rose rapidly to manage the new Edinburgh factory and then establish another plant in London.

When McVitie died in 1920, Grant gained control of the company. Its tremendous growth was fed by the growing urban population, hungry for variety and convenient snacks to eat in the tea parlors that were springing up everywhere. With Grant as chairman and managing director, McVitie & Price became a world leader. Following his success, Grant turned to philanthropy, helping found the National Library for Scotland. Grant was awarded a baronetcy in 1924, and while there were questions of undue influence, Grant maintained his role as a financial leader.

7

Clans

Roman chroniclers called the Celtic tribes Caledonians or Picts. Meanwhile, the Norsemen overran not only the western isles but much of the northern part of the country. For a time it was an even chance whether ancient Caledonia would become Norseland or Scotland. Under Malcolm Canmore and his sons, however, the Scots pushed their conquests south of the Forth, annexed Strathclyde, Northumberland, and Westmoreland, and became a formidable power in the land.

The clan system developed largely from the mountainous nature of the country in which the people lived, each family or tribe living in its own glen, separate from the rest of the world, and too remote to be interfered with by a central government. In these circumstances, as in similar circumstances elsewhere—Afghanistan and Arabia, for instance—the father of the family became the ruler, and when the family grew into a tribe he became its chief. In later days, when great combinations of re-

lated clans were formed, the chief of the strongest branch might become captain of the confederacy, like the captain of Clanranald and the captain of clan Chattan. The chiefship was inherited by the eldest legitimate son, but it must be remembered that in the Highlands the son of a "handfast" union was considered legitimate, whether his parents married or not. (Handfasting was a form of trial marriage lasting for a year and a day. If it proved unfruitful it could be terminated at the end of that time. Sometimes a chief might die or be slain before his handfast union could be confirmed by marriage, and in this case his son was still recognized as heir.) The clan system arose from the urgent need to carry on the direct line of the chiefs.

A chief portioned out his lands to his sons as tenants. When his eldest son succeeded as chief, the new chief portioned out the lands to his own sons in the same way. Thus the nearest relatives of the chief were always the men of highest rank and most influence in the clan, while the oldest cadets, unless they had secured their positions in time by their own exertions, were apt to find their way into the ranks of the ordinary clansmen. As all clansmen claimed descent from the house of the chief, all prided themselves upon the rank of gentleman, and being a Scottish Highlander was an important badge of honor.

Today clans are important to Scots in tracing their family histories. Most Scots feel they belong to a clan, something that shows up in Scottish-American festivals, sometimes dominated by particular clans.

Clan insignias, colors, and tartans are very important, and each clan's role in the formation of Scotland is a source of pride to descendents of Scottish clans, often recognized by their last names, such as Campbell, McGowan, McGregor, and Stewart.

8

Curling

Scots and continental Europeans both claim to be founders of the sport of curling. Did Scots invent the game, or was it imported by Flemish sportsmen who immigrated to Scotland during the reign of James VI (James I of England)? Did Europeans engage in some early form of curling, and did Scots merely adopt and enhance it? The evidence, based on works of art, contemporary writings, and archaeological finds, has sparked a number of theories, but none is conclusive. To add to the puzzle, archaeological evidence—a curling stone (the famous Stirling Stone) inscribed with the date 1511—turned up, along with another stone bearing the date 1551, when an old pond was drained at Dunblane, Scotland.

Two oil paintings by the Dutch master Pieter Brueghel, entitled "Winter Landscape with Skaters and a Birdtrap" and "Hunters in the Snow," created in 1565, show *eisschiessen* or "ice shooting," a Bavarian game played with a long sticklike handle that is still enjoyed today.

Another work, an engraving by R. de Baudous (1575–1644), shows players who appear to be sliding large discs of wood along a frozen waterway. Other sketches from around the same time show a Dutch game called *kuting*, played with frozen lumps of earth.

The first handwritten record of what could be called an early curling game dates from February 1540, when John McQuhin of Scotland noted down, in Latin, a challenge to a game on ice between a monk named John Sclater and an associate, Gavin Hamilton. The first printed reference to curling appears in a seventeenth-century elegy published by Henry Adamson, following the death of a close friend: "His name was M. James Gall, a citizen of Perth, and a gentle-man of goodly stature, and pregnant wit, much given to pastime, as golf, archerie, curling and jovial companie." It seems that the game tempted many people from all walks of life. Records from a Glasgow Assembly of Presbyterians in 1638 accused a certain Bishop Graham of Orkney of a terrible act: He was curling on the ice on the Sabbath.

There is no doubt that if the Scots did not invent curling, they made the game what it is today. They improved the equipment and established rules. In 1760, Scottish troops melted down cannonballs to fashion curling irons. By the eighteenth century, curling had become a common pastime in Scotland. The Duddingston Club first set out the "Rules in Curling" in 1804, which were similar to those followed today. Subsequently, as more and more clubs were formed, it became evident

that a governing body had to be set up to coordinate the growth of the curling community, at least in Scotland. John Cairnie was an accomplished curler who had built a curling hall at Largs in 1813. He was also an innovator and the driving force for the creation of a "Mother Club of Curling." In 1833, he called on all Scottish clubs to submit lists of their officers, numbers of curlers, and matches played. The information was used to establish the Grand Caledonian Curling Club in Edinburgh in 1838, and to provide for its members *The Annuals,* a record of curling that has been compiled regularly since 1839.

In 1843, the Grand Caledonian was granted the patronage of Prince Albert, and was renamed the Royal Caledonian Curling Club. Since then, patrons have always been members of the royal family, and, beginning in 1900, have been either a king or a queen. The founding of the Royal Club gave curling its first central association, and the occasion is generally considered as the most prominent and far-reaching event in the history of the sport.

Scottish immigrants introduced curling to Canada, where it thrived and attained a level of excellence that remains unsurpassed. Long, harsh Canadian winters were ideal for the game. By 1807, the first North American club was established when twenty sporting Montreal merchants, who had been curling on the ice of the St. Lawrence River behind Molson's Brewery, founded the Montreal Curling Club, which became known in 1924 as the Royal Montreal Curling Club.

9

Distilleries

No one really knows exactly when Scotch whisky (the Scottish spelling) was first distilled. In fact, the origins of distilling itself are generally obscure, although it was first attempted in Asia as long ago as 800 B.C., and may have found its way to Europe via Egypt.

The ancient Celts practiced the art of distilling spirits and had an expressive name for the fiery liquid they produced: *uisge beatha*—the water of life. To the Celts its power to revive tired bodies and failing spirits, to drive out chills and rekindle hope, was a veritable gift from God. Regardless of its beginnings, the Scots have perfected the art of distilling, using the elements so generously provided for them by nature. Whisky is inextricably woven into Scotland's history, culture, and customs. The earliest documented record of distilling in Scotland occurred in 1494, when an entry in the Exchequer Rolls listed "Eight bolls of malt to Friar John Cor wherewith to make *aqua vitae* (water of life)."

This was sufficient to produce almost 1500 bottles. Thus, it is clear that distilling was already a well-established practice. Primitive equipment was used initially, but by the sixteenth and seventeenth centuries distillation became more sophisticated. The dissolution of the monasteries contributed to the growth of the distilling industry, since many of the monks turned to distilling for their livelihood. The knowledge of distilling then quickly spread.

The increasing popularity of whisky eventually attracted the attention of the Scottish parliament, which introduced the first taxes on malt and whisky in the latter part of the seventeenth century. Ever increasing rates of taxation were applied following The Act of Union with England in 1707, when England set out to tame the rebellious clans of Scotland. The distillers were virtually driven underground. Smuggling became standard practice for some 150 years and there was no moral stigma attached to it. Ministers of the church made storage space available under the pulpit, and the illicit spirit was, on occasion, transported by coffin. Any effective means was used to escape the government's capture of whisky.

By 1777, a mere eight licensed distilleries contributed to the revenue of the United Kingdom in the City of Edinburgh, while nearly 400 unregistered stills were said to be contributing only to the personal gains of the bootleggers who ran them. This was in any case miniscule when compared to the operations of illicit distillers in the remote Highlands and islands of Scotland.

This flouting of the law eventually prompted the Duke of Gordon, on whose extensive acres some of the finest illicit whisky in Scotland was being produced, to propose in the House of Lords that the government should make it profitable to produce whisky legally. In 1823 the Excise Act was passed, which sanctioned the distilling of whisky in return for a license fee and a set payment per gallon of proof spirit. This law gave birth to the Scotch whisky industry. Smuggling died out almost completely over the next ten years and, in fact, a great many of the present-day distilleries stand on sites originally used by smugglers.

Glenturret Distillery is the oldest single highland malt distillery in Scotland. It was established in 1775, but dates back to 1717, when there were numerous "bothies" (a type of farm) in Glenturret. It is believed that there were as many as five on the distillery site—all had "illicit stills" and drew their water from the Turret Burn. Glenturret Distillery was originally in the hands of smugglers who brought the whisky to England to avoid paying taxes. The distillery site was selected not only for its convenient slope to the river but also because there were high hills on either side, which provided excellent lookout points for the smugglers.

Today the Scottish tourism industry promotes visits to two whisky trails. The best known is the Speyside Malt Whisky Trail, which is about 70 miles in length and takes in the distilleries of Tamnavulin, Glenlivet, Glenfarclas, Tamdhu, Cardhu, Glen Grant, Strathisla, Glenfiddich, and

the Speyside Cooperage at Craigellachie. Less well known is the Islay and Jura Whisky Trail, which takes in Caol Ila, Bunnahabhain, Bruichladdich, Bowmore, Ardbeg, Lagavulin, Laphroaig, and Isle of Jura.

One of the oldest bottles of single-malt whisky in the world recently set a record price at auction. The 62-year-old Dalmore whisky was bought by an anonymous bidder in Glasgow for approximately $40,627, which works out to about $1,500 a shot. The Dalmore is one of only twelve bottles made at the company's Scottish distillery in Alness, with each bottle named after an important event or character in the history of the distillery. The bottle sold was named Kildermorie after the lake that supplies the distillery's water.

10

Edinburgh Festival

The highlight of Scotland's calendar is the Edinburgh Festival, held every August. This is one of the world's most important arts festivals, with over 500 performers every year. The city's Military Tattoo is held at the same time.

The Edinburgh International Festival was founded in 1947. Performance at the festival is by invitation only, issued by the festival director. It is now recognized as one of the most important celebrations of the arts in the world, and is so important to Scottish tourism that it is sponsored by the Bank of Scotland and many Scottish businesses. My visit to the festival was the highlight of my trip to Edinburgh.

From its early days, the Edinburgh Tattoo has been an international favorite. Today it draws an audience of over 200,000, 35 percent of them from overseas. The Tattoo has been televised in 30 countries, and an annual television audience of 100 million watches the coverage world-

wide. There are usually five or six pipe bands performing in the Edinburgh Tattoo. The infantry battalions of the Scottish Division are always well represented and the regular services provide at least one other band—sometimes from the Guards, the Cavalry, the Gurkhas, or the Royal Air Force. The musicians in these bands are all fighting servicemen for whom combat must take priority over piping and drumming. In the infantry, for example, the pipe band usually has the official role of battalion machine gun platoon. Virtually all senior British military pipers have attended the Army School of Piping, as have many pipers from overseas contingents. The fact that so many musicians have attained such high standards is all the more impressive when one considers that the school has a staff of only two. Its director is also the director of army bagpipe music; his only colleague at the school is its pipe major and chief instructor. The school, based in Edinburgh Castle, was founded in 1910. Among its regular courses are a seven-month pipe majors' course and a three-week, class-one pipers' course. Since 1981, it has been in charge of the Edinburgh Military Tattoo, selecting some of the pipe bands from the British services, putting together the program of pipe music, and directing the overall performance.

11

Gardens and Woodlands

Tourists in Scotland can't resist its castles, but its many gardens are also popular sites. They range from the Glasgow botanical garden to the biblical garden in Elgin, from the subtropical garden in Inverness to the famous woodland of Achamore Gardens.

Although situated at a latitude north of Moscow, Cawdor Castle's fertile soil, located in a climate tempered by the Gulf stream—lots of rainfall, and summer sun—supports three famous gardens. The Walled Garden is the oldest. It dates from about 1600, and was enclosed with walls in 1620. By 1635, there were records of cultivated orchards of fruit and vegetables. The Flower Garden was laid out around 1710 by the Thane of Cawdor's brother, who was at that time manager of the family estates in Scotland. The Thane himself had studied in France and requested that French design be used in the garden. In the nineteenth century, the family generally stayed at Cawdor only during the summer and

fall, when lavender borders enclosed showy summer rose beds. The Wild Garden is the youngest, planted in the twentieth century and filled with informal plants and nature trails through mixed woodlands. The Big Wood at Cawdor is a must-see and still contains the remnants of the classic dry oakwood, including birch, aspen, rowan, wych elm, holly and juniper, Scots pine, oak, and beech.

The old castle of Dummond has a fine nineteenth-century garden that includes a sundial from the 1630s carved by Charles I's master mason. Drummond castle is set on a ridge with terraces that step down the hill to the south. A large parterre takes the form of Scotland's flag, the St. Andrew's cross, centered on the old sundial.

Adjacent to Elgin Cathedral lies a biblical garden, the first of its kind in Scotland. All 110 plants mentioned in the Bible are planted around sculptures depicting the parables. A desert area depicting Mount Sinai has been created, and the cave of the resurrection has been included within the garden. Halfway between Grantown-on-Spey and the Boat of Garten is the Speyside Heather Garden. Here you can see over 300 varieties of heather. Glendurgan, a woodland garden in a deep valley with collections of rhododendrons and camellias, has an interesting maze, planted in 1833 by Alfred Fox.

The once extensive Caledonian Forest of Scotland has been almost completely destroyed over the past thousand years to provide pine logs for the construction and boat-building industries. Scattered remnants

of Scotland's original Caledonian forest can still be found in a few places, such as Glen Affric and Rothiemurchus.

The Scots pine is still an important timber species in Britain. Pine needles, together with those of non-native spruce, are used in the production of specialty beers, a practice originally introduced by the Vikings. A small number of contemporary Scottish basket makers also make delicate ornamental baskets using pine needles. The resin-rich roots of the pine tree were used as candles prior to the introduction of oil lamps.

12

Ghosts, Witches, Superstitions, and Hubble-Bubble

Ghosts are everywhere in Scotland, from Duncan's ghost in *Macbeth* to the ghost of Stirling Castle, a woman in a long pink dress.

Edinburgh Castle is haunted by the ghost of a headless drummer who is said to appear only when the castle is about to be besieged. His first recorded appearance was in 1650 just before Cromwell attacked. A one-armed ghost reputedly haunts Dalry House in Edinburgh. The spirit is supposedly that of John Chiesly, a man who had his arm chopped off as punishment for shooting Sir George Lockhart.

Walter Scott's "Bride of Lammermoor" was based on real events in Baldoon Castle, Dumfries, and to this day the bloodstained ghost of the bride, who was either murdered or driven insane according to different versions of the tale, is said to haunt the castle. Arnish Moor on the Isle

of Lewis was haunted by a figure dressed in eighteenth-century clothing. The body of a similar figure was dug from the moor in 1964, and since then—as spooky as it may seem—the appearances of the ghost have ceased.

In Sandwick, in the Orkley Islands, it is said that on certain nights the ghostly White Horse of Clumly and its rider haunt the area, reenacting the events of a dark night many years ago. Several people have reported seeing a large white horse and rider leap over the wall to the sound of falling stones.

According to Scottish tradition, the sound of a dog barking or howling in the night signals an impending death. At the holiday of Martinmas, the crowing of a cockerel, especially a black one, was thought to frighten away evil spirits. The many stone circles and neolithic graves all over Scotland are surrounded by legends of clan chiefs and giants. The line of stones near Dun are called the Howhane Shearers, said to be people who were turned to stone.

Foxglove was included in a love charm in the late nineteenth century; it had to be burned to ashes with butterbur, seaweed, royal fern, and an old man's bones on a flat stone at the shore. The ashes were then sprinkled on the loved one's chest, ensuring he would never leave.

One of Scotland's most notorious witches was Isobel Gowdie, who claimed during her trial in 1662 that she had made a pact with the devil

fifteen years earlier that enabled her to fly and turn into a cat. The area around St. Andrews was once known as a center of witchcraft, and Witch Hill was where many of the accused were burned. In 1623, a Scottish woman named Isobel Haldane was tried for witchcraft and confessed to associating with fairy folk. Scotland's last witch trial was in 1722, when Janet Horne was sentenced to death by burning in a tar barrel.

The most frightening Scottish horror story is a true one. In Scotland, medical students were accustomed to using real cadavers for their studies. Officially, each medical school was allotted only one executed criminal per year. This did not meet the demands of the anatomy students, so there arose rumors of a sinister trade of "body snatchers." As early as 1738, it was recorded that bodies were leaving graveyards to appear in Edinburgh Medical School laboratories. Unfortunately, the suspected body snatchers were often the medical students themselves. This practice so horrified the general public that watchtowers were constructed in some Edinburgh graveyards to protect those recently buried from exhumation. In addition to the towers, protective walls and iron bars can still be seen around some old Edinburgh graveyards.

In 1828, the trial of one of Edinburgh's most distinguished surgeons, Dr. Robert Knox, revealed that he had made arrangements with two criminals, William Burke and William Hare (who may have actually been Irish), to obtain cadavers from various Edinburgh cemeteries.

Burke and Hare were extremely enterprising. Rather than waiting for signs of a burial, they lured the homeless and vagrant into traps, killed them, and sold their bodies to Dr. Knox. The trial of Burke and Hare became famous throughout Britain.

13

Golf

There is a saying that the people of St. Andrews do nothing but play golf, but this cannot be true, as St. Andrews has one of the four great Scottish universities. No one has definitively proved that the Scots were responsible for inventing the game of golf but, like distilling whisky, they can take the credit for its development. The Romans played a variation of the game, using balls stuffed with feathers that they hit with club-shaped branches. Both the French and the Dutch have tried to claim the invention of golf with their ball-and-stick games—the Dutch played a version of golf on ice in the fifteenth century—but their sports did not include golf's most important ingredient: the hole. Driving a tiny ball through innumerable obstacles to eventally drop it into a tiny hole is a uniquely Scottish invention.

Golf was being played on the eastern coast of Scotland by the fifteenth century, possibly as early as the Middle Ages. An early Scottish story

claims that local shepherds in the St. Andrews area were hitting round stones into rabbit burrows using their wooden crooks.

The Scottish Parliament passed an act in 1457 banning the playing of golf. It was interfering with archery practice and this proved detrimental to the nation's defenses. King James IV tried to ban golf as well, but was instead converted to the game, and Scottish monarchs were avid players ever after—even Mary Queen of Scots was a golfer during her brief reign.

By the beginning of the seventeenth century, golf had spread throughout all of Scotland and was enjoyed not only by the nobility but the common folk as well. The Robertson family can be traced back to Thomas Buddo, a ballmaker in St. Andrews in 1610. His daughter married a Robertson and from this pair was bred the stock that produced generations of ballmakers. At least four distinct Robertson families were engaged in making balls in St. Andrews in the mid-eighteenth century. During this same century, the game was properly organized with accepted rules for all players. In 1744, the Gentlemen Golfers of Leith, later renamed the Honourable Company of Edinburgh Golfers, was instituted. The Royal and Ancient Golf Club of St. Andrews was founded in 1754.

From 1750 to 1850, golf developed into the game we know today. It was during this time that the great golf clubs were founded and talented players started to gain renown. Great players gathered for "meetings" in

which medal and matchplay rounds were organized, and distinctions between amateur and professional players were made for the first time. Allan Robertson is credited as the first golf professional, but before him, his grandfather Peter Robertson, who died in 1803, was described as a professional golfer and his prowess was widely acknowledged.

Golf exploded onto the international scene in the late 1800s, following the invention of the gutta percha ball by James Patterson in 1848. Patterson, a member of a university family, experimented with the rubbery material that had arrived as packaging material for a statuette sent to him from Malaya. The feather-filled balls used up until that time were not only expensive, they were also unpredictable and disappeared in the wind. The new ball was more durable and made it possible to use more iron shots in the game. Then in 1852, the railway came to St. Andrews and with it the first of the millions of golfers who have made the pilgrimage since. Soon the links were played all year round, and the University of St. Andrews achieved a stature comparable to Oxford and Cambridge; rich families began settling there for their sons' educations as well as for the sport of golf.

It was during this same period that Tommy Morris, the game's greatest exponent, revolutionized golf with the new iron clubs he made in St. Andrews, clubs that would gain him success and raise the standards of the game. Irons that were previously used only for a bad lie were now used for driving, lofting, and putting. Famous golfers like

Douglas Rolland and his nephew James Braid, Sandy Herd, the Kirkcaldy brothers, and the Dunne twins made Scotland the center of golf. Harry Vardon came from the Channel Island of Jersey and Henry Taylor from Bridgeport in Devon. Scottish golfers began crossing the Atlantic to enjoy the spoils of the newly emerged game of golf in the United States. The early U.S. Open champions were all Scottish-born players who, as teachers and mentors, produced players who would further transform the game. They also played an important role in golf course design, now a major industry.

Although golf is now an international game, The Royal and Ancient Golf Club of St. Andrews holds a unique position as a leading authority in the world. It administers the Rules of Golf, in conjunction with the United States Golf Association, and oversees the running of the open championship and other key events. In 1996, the Scottish Golf Union established the Scottish National Golf Centre at Drumoig, eight miles northwest of St. Andrews. Most serious golfers dream of vacationing in Scotland and trying out some of the world's finest courses.

14

Great American Scots

While some Scots arrived in America with nothing but a willingness to work hard, many Scottish immigrants were highly skilled artisans, craftsmen, merchants, and teachers and, later on, engineers, scientists, and inventors. For the most part, they were well educated and literate, as has been true in most of Scotland for a very long time. The Scots have added immeasurably to the culture and prosperity of the United States. In his book *The Mark of the Scots,* Duncan Bruce points out that, as of 1993, of the twenty-one largest charitable foundations in the U.S.—boasting assets of over $25 billion—Scottish Americans started thirteen.

Among the most famous immigrants were the industrialists Andrew Carnegie, who made his money from railroads and Pittsburgh steel; and John D. Rockefeller, the first person in America to make a for-

tune out of oil. His company, Standard Oil, became the largest industrial corporation in the world. Like Andrew Carnegie, Rockefeller devoted the later years of his life to establishing charitable corporations with donations estimated at between $530 million and $750 million. The University of Chicago, the first major recipient of his largesse, received a total of $35 million. His son John Davison Rockefeller, Jr., who worked closely with him, continued the tradition of philanthropy, contributing a further $400 million to charitable causes. The Rockefeller Foundation remains one of America's largest foundations.

Andrew William Mellon, an American banker and politician born in 1855, was one of the three or four wealthiest men of his time. In 1921, he was appointed Secretary of the Treasury. He founded an art college and funded the Mellon Institute in Pittsburgh for Scientific Research.

More recent millionaire and billionaire philanthropists have included the legendary oil magnate and founder of Getty Oil, J. Paul Getty, at one time the richest man in the U.S. and probably the world. His roots were modest; on his mother's side, Getty's ancestors fled Scotland after the Battle of Culloden. On his father's side, his ancestors were Ulster Scots Presbyterians who founded Gettysburg, Pennsylvania. Getty set up charitable foundations worth hundreds of millions and his son, John Paul Getty II, who now lives in England, has continued the tradition. Another significant modern-day philanthropist is the billion-

aire founder of Microsoft, William (Bill) H. Gates III, who is of Scottish descent through his mother.

Many of the Founding Fathers of America came from Scotland. They were so important in American history that they are grouped together in a special Scots in American History section. They included many of the signers of the Declaration of Independence and some of our early presidents.

Alexander Wilson, a Scottish immigrant, was the author of seven volumes of American ornithology, and Dr. Benjamin Waterhouse, a graduate of Edinburgh University, helped found Harvard Medical School. Allan Pinkerton, born in Gorbals, Glasgow in 1819, left Scotland hurriedly in 1842 following his involvement in left-wing protests. In 1852, in Chicago, he formed the first detective agency (which still exists nationwide today), and solved a series of train robberies. In 1861, while guarding President Abraham Lincoln on his way to his inauguration he foiled an assassination plot in Baltimore. Pinkerton was the head of the U.S. Secret Service in 1861 and 1862.

Many Civil War figures were either born in Scotland or claimed Scottish heritage. Jefferson Davis, the president of the Confederate States of America, was of Scottish descent, as were Confederate generals Joseph Johnston, John Brown Gordon, John B. Magruder, John C. Breckenridge, and George Whythe Randolph. The famous Union general Ambrose Burnside was also a Scot.

Writer Robert Louis Stevenson immigrated to the United States in 1879, and published an account of the crossing, *The Amateur Emigrant*, in 1883. A moving account of an immigrant ship sailing from Lochaber in the mid-eighteenth century appears in his novel *Kidnapped.* Washington Irving, the American author of "Rip Van Winkle" and other classics, was also of Scottish descent.

Thomas Duncan was born in Drumrann Farm, to the northeast of Girvan in Ayrshire, in 1865. He was apprenticed to a local pharmacist before leaving home and emigrating to the United States. His first employment on arrival in the U.S. in 1882 was in a Boston, Massachusetts, drugstore. After a short return to Scotland, he returned to the United States and was hired by the Sun Electrical Company of Woburn, Massachusetts. From there he moved on to the Jenny Electric Light Company in Fort Wayne, Indiana, as superintendent of the incandescent lamp department. Duncan was interested in methods for the measurement of electricity. To pursue his interest in this field, he took a pay cut and joined the Thompson Houston Electric Company of Lynn, Massachusetts—the forerunner of the General Electric Company.

In 1890, Duncan returned to the Fort Wayne Electric Company as head of the laboratory and testing department, and in 1892 he applied for a patent for his first electric meter. Four years later, the Fort Wayne Company was manufacturing thousands of the Duncan meters. In 1901, Thomas Duncan established his own Duncan Electric Manufac-

turing Company in Lafayette, Indiana, and by 1928 the company was employing about 500 people to meet the worldwide demand for electric meters. Many important innovations in meters are credited to Thomas Duncan, who is regarded as the founder of the electric meter industry.

David Jacks, controversial landowner and dairy farmer in Monterey County, California, and the popularizer of Monterey Jack, one of America's favorite cheeses, was born in Crieff. Henry Wallace, Secretary of Agriculture under Franklin D. Roosevelt, was the grandson of a Scottish Presbyterian minister. Robert Gibson Eccles, a Scot from Ayrshire was one of the discoverers of food preservatives. John McLaren, a Scot from Bannockburn, created the Garden of the Golden Gate in San Francisco. John MacIntosh, who developed the Macintosh apple, (the edible one) was the son of a Scot from Inverness.

15

Handfasting and Other Scottish Customs

In late-medieval and early-modern Scotland (and northern England), "handfasting" was the term used for "betrothal," the ceremony of exchanging future consents to marriage and agreeing to marriage contracts. Among the Highland clans, it was considered an important way of cementing family unions. Even if the handfasting did not lead to marriage, any children were considered the legitimate children of the union—an important factor in the ascendancy of clan chiefs.

Handfasting remained legal in Scotland all the way up to 1939, even after Lord Harwicke's Act of 1753, which declared that marriages in England were legal only if performed by a clergyman. After Lord Harwicke's Act, the Scottish border town of Gretna Green became a mecca for eloping couples from England, who fled there to perform their own

handfastings. In those times, the couple themselves performed the handfasting before witnesses. It was also used in Scotland for the engagement period of a year and a day before a wedding was finalized.

The word handfasting has its origin in the wedding custom of tying the bride and groom's hands (actually, wrists) together. In some versions, this is only done for as long as the ceremony lasts, but in others, the cord is not untied until the marriage is physically consummated. Today handfasting rituals are a favorite of practitioners of wiccan, pagan, and other alternative spiritual practices.

Another Scottish tradition dictates that on Midsummer's Eve, one should wear a short tunic-style shirt with nothing underneath. (Is this the origin of the mystery of what is worn underneath a kilt?) Kilts are also traditionally worn for festivals and Highland Games.

Although the official flower of Scotland is the bluebell, thistle is thought to have special powers. The Order of the Thistle, founded in 1470, is Scotland's oldest order of knights.

16

Heather

The name Heather, most commonly used for this plant (and my own first name!) is of Scottish origin. It presumably derived from the Scots word *haeddre*, and has been recorded as far back as the fourteenth century. The word has many variations: *hader* is found in Old Scottish from 1399, *heddir* from 1410, *hathar* from 1597 (although this form of the word may also be seen in place names dating back to 1094), and finally *heather* from 1584.

Heather moors cover a vast amount of the Scottish countryside, approximately two to three million acres in the East and only slightly fewer in the South and West. It is without doubt one of Scotland's most prolific and abundant plants. While Scotland may be more famous for its whisky than for its beer, the first recorded alcoholic drink produced in the country was heather ale, believed to have been made by the Picts.

Each tiny heather flower has thirty seeds, so it is quite possible for

one large plant to produce up to 150,000 seeds per season. Wind and weather, insects, and even heavy grazing by cattle and sheep do not easily damage heather. It flourishes in temperatures as low as 18° F in winter and as high as 100° F in summer.

As one of the most common and readily available resources in the countryside, heather has always played an important role in the traditional construction of buildings, particularly in areas such as the Hebridean Islands where it was used to build houses, churches, and farms. From walls, roofs, and even the ropes and pegs, which actually held the buildings together, thatching with heather was common in areas as far apart as Shetland in the North and the Island of Arran in the Southwest. Houses on the island of Mull were constructed by wattling together heather and branches of wood. In Strathspey, it has been recorded that heather brushwood was used (in conjunction with wild juniper) inside walls of houses to act as insulation and soundproofing. The Skara Brae excavation in Orkney revealed a prehistoric village dating back to around 2,000 B.C., and among the primitive tools and animal bones they discovered *Seomain fraoich*—heather rope, used for beds. Heather had many practical uses, from baskets and brushes to pot scrubbers, brooms, and doormats.

The healing properties of heather have been recorded as far back as the Middle Ages, and there are books on using heather and other herbs dating even further back, to the seventh century. A German book, writ-

ten in 1565, describes the famous doctor Paulus Aegineta using the flowers, leaves, and stems to heal all types of sores, incuding ulcers, internal and external. Heather also seemed to heal insect bites, snakebites, eye infections, and infections of the spleen, as well as to prevent the formation of stones in internal organs. Nicolas Alexandre, a Benedictine monk, wrote that boiling heather stems and drinking the liquid for thirty consecutive days, morning and evening, was sufficient to dissolve kidney stones. He added that the patient should also bathe in the heather water. Since 1930, heather, referred to by the medical profession as Herba Callunae, has been acknowledged by many doctors and chemists to be effective against arthritis, spleen complaints, the formation of stones, stomach and backaches, and even paralysis and tuberculosis. This remarkable plant is also known to be good for sore throats, gout, catarrh, and coughs. Some say it even cleanses the blood, getting rid of eczema and fevers. Pure heather honey is recommended for hay fever sufferers.

17

Highland Games

Scottish Festivals and Highland Games are not only popular in Scotland, but are also held all over the United States. These include the original sports contests for adults and children, and other events such as clan gatherings, clan blessings, dancing, food, and bagpipe playing. They are also an opportunity to show various Scottish traditions and sell products.

The games are typically quite challenging, recalling the very physical nature of contests in medieval Europe. Turning the caber is an old game. This is an attempt to hold a heavy log (about 100 pounds) vertically, run forward, and throw the log so that it spins to the ground, pointing straight away from the player. The sheaf toss involves throwing a twenty-pound bag of hay up in the air with a pitchfork. The highest toss wins. There are also many weight throws involving stones of various weights, thrown both high and far. In the hammer throw, a metal

ball is attached to a wooden handle, creating a hammer. Battleax throws are replicas of contests held among the Highlands military regiments. In the farmer's walk, each athlete walks with about 100 pounds of weight on each arm. The traditional tug-of-war has a Scottish twist that requires all participants to be kilted; the same goes for golf matches and track events. Game participants also play a form of rugby that comes from the Borders area of Scotland. Some Highland Games include fly-fishing contests.

The town of Ceres in Fife claims to hold the oldest Highland Games in Scotland. Since 1314, the Ceres Games have been held each June to commemorate the safe return of Ceres men from the Battle of Bannockburn.

Bute is one of the larger amateur Highland Games, held each August in Rothesay on the Firth of Clyde Island of Bute. Rothesay is probably the most famous and best loved of all the holiday towns on the Firth of Clyde. The road to the games field runs past the massive red sandstone structure of Rothesay Castle, parts of which date back to the thirteenth century. The playing area is on a local field that has a substantial hill. Not surprisingly, many of the leading amateur throwers have their seasonal best performances at Bute.

18

Hogmany and Other Scottish Festivals

The Scottish New Year, known as *Hogmany,* is traditionally celebrated on December 31. One of the old rituals was a thorough house cleaning, a form of purification that included carrying burning juniper branches around the house to remove disease. Traditional food and drink for Hogmany include haggis, shortbread, scones, oatcakes, cheese, black buns, whisky, and wine. Bonfires also represent the disposing of the old year. After midnight people wait to see who their first visitor will be—it was believed that the arrival of a dark-haired man with a small gift brought good luck. Robert Burns's *Auld Lang Syne* is sung not only in Scotland but all over the world as a mark of the end of the old year and the beginning of the new.

Hallowe'en, or *Samhnag,* from the earliest Celtic records, has been

the most important and sinister festival of the Celtic year. It was originally celebrated on the night of November 1 and on the following day. On this day, it was thought that the pagan gods and spirits became visible to humans. There were many rituals designed to save ordinary people from the mischief of these beings. *Samhnag* is still observed but the old significance has been lost. Different parts of the Highlands still carry on their own traditional activities, but these are less authentic and varied as the old beliefs and traditional ways of celebrating rapidly disappear.

In certain regions of the Highlands, the *Samhnag* "bonfire" was a communal effort, and it was built on the mound known as *Càrn nam Marbh,* "The Mound of the Dead." According to tradition, the mound contained the bodies of victims of a dreadful plague, brought there and buried by an old woman with a cart or sled pulled by a white horse. A stone, known as *Clach a' Phlàigh,* "the Plague Stone," crowned the mound.

In other places bonfires were lit, and it was usually the children who built them. After sunset, in many places, every youth who was able to carry a blazing torch or *Samhnag* ran out and circuited the boundaries of their farms with these blazing brands in order to protect the family possessions from the fairies and all other malevolent forces. Then, having secured their homes in this manner, by the purifying force of the sacred fire, all the households in a township would gather together and participate in the traditional activities. Nuts and apples were regularly

served. In the Hebrides the boys dressed up in disguises and went from house to house; much damage to property was done by them on this wild night—gates removed, carts overturned, and other types of things typically done on mischief night in America.

The feast of St. Martin was held on November 11, one of the Scottish quarter days. It is usually referred to as Martinmas but pronounced Martimas. It was the same day as Hallowe'en in the old calendar.

Saint Andrew was adopted as the patron saint of Scotland after a famous Pictish victory in 747 A.D. during the reign of Aengus. His relics are believed to be at St. Andrews. There were attempts to set up an observance day, and King James IV celebrated it with a Saint Andrew's Dinner. Traps were set for rabbits and squirrels and the farmworkers set off to the woods on what was known as "going Sanct Andra-ing." They brought the game home to be cooked, and the feasting included much drinking. St. Andrew's Day is a day celebrated more often abroad by expatriots than in Scotland. St Andrew's societies in many parts of the world hold dinners on the night of November 30. They wear tartan and the kilt, sing Scottish songs, and dance Scottish reels and strathspeys.

In folklore there are four "quarter days" of the year, often called the four "Lesser Sabbats," or the four "Low Holidays." The summer solstice is one of them. The summer solstice occurs when the sun reaches the Tropic of Cancer, and we experience the longest day and the shortest night of the year. The celebration is on its eve, or the sunset immediately

preceding the solstice point. Again, it gives modern pagans a range of dates to choose from with, they hope, a weekend embedded in it. In England, it was the ancient custom to light large bonfires after sundown, which served the double purpose of providing light to the revelers and warding off evil spirits. This was known as "setting the watch." People often jumped through the fires for good luck. In addition to these fires, the streets were lined with lanterns, and people carried them from one bonfire to another. These wandering, garland-bedecked bands were called a "marching watch." Often they were accompanied by morris dancers and traditional players dressed, respectfully, as a unicorn, a dragon, and six hobby-horse riders. According to British fairy lore, this night was second only to Halloween for its importance to the wee folk. Other customs included decking the house (especially over the front door) with birch, fennel, St. John's wort, orpin, and white lillies.

19

Kilts and Sporrans

The kilt is seen as the national dress of Scotland. There's an expression that "a man in a kilt is a man and a half."

The Highland Scots emigrated from Ireland around 375. A.D. They displaced the native Picts and brought Irish dress from their homeland. This consisted of a *léine* (pronounced lay-na) and a *brat. Léine* is the modern Irish word for shirt. In antiquity, the *léine* was similar to a linen undertunic, although silk is occasionally mentioned. It was usually white or unbleached, often decorated with red or gold embroidery at the neck and cuffs, and sometimes hooded as well. A woman wore it long; a man's *léine* ended at his knees. In the earliest times, the *léine* probably had no shape at all. However, in the Norman era, it gained definition in the waist.

The earliest authentic mention of the kilt appears to be in the Norse history of Magnus Barefoot, with whom Malcolm Canmore made his

famous treaty. According to that document, written around the year 1097, Magnus, upon returning from his conquest of the Hebrides, adopted the dress in use there, and went about bare-legged, wearing a short tunic and also an upper garment. John Major, a fifteenth-century historian, noted that the Highland gentlemen of his day "wore no covering from the middle of the thigh to the foot, clothing themselves with a mantle instead of an upper garment, and a shirt dyed with saffron." By the Elizabethan age, it had become a full-pleated smock made from at least seven yards of fabric. It was always made of linen and its color was invariably yellow. The English referred to it as the "saffron shirt" and in 1537 Henry VIII banned its use in Ireland (saffron was, and still is, a very expensive spice; its use as a dye was a luxury reserved for nobility, not the common Irish). By this time, the *léine* had also developed long, draping sleeves. It has been pictured as long and flowing, the length hitched up over a belt. Other depictions, particularly in Ulster and the islands nearest Scotland, portray it as reaching only to mid-thigh, with wide sleeves and an elaborately pleated skirt like a short kilt. However, it was never made of wool or plaid material.

The *brat* is a rectangular piece of cloth thrown around the body and fastened on the breast or shoulder by a brooch. Both men and women wore them. The *brat* could be wrapped around the shoulders or looped under the sword arm for better maneuverability. *Brats* were worn in varying lengths depending upon the occasion and the rank of the

wearer. Some tales speak of the Queen's *brat* dragging on the ground behind her chariot. They were also worn in many colors; a brat with many colors was a sign of nobility.

The *sporran,* held by a chain strap, sits at the center of the front apron of the kilt and is required to be worn with it. The sporran ranges in style and material, but you will never see a pipe band without them.

Claims have been made that an Englishman named Rawlinson who was in charge of an iron-smelting works in Lochaber devised the modern kilt. Needless to say, the Scots vigorously deny this.

20

Lighthouses

Robert Stevenson, the grandfather of Robert Louis Stevenson, was as famous as his grandson, but as an engineer rather than a writer. Stevenson and his family designed and built many of Scotland's lighthouses. Born in Glasgow in 1772, he was a young engineer when his stepfather, Thomas Smith, entrusted him with the building of Pentland Skerries Lighthouse. Stevenson became his stepfather's partner and then became chief engineer of the Northern Lighthouse Board from 1808 until 1842. During his term, he was responsible for the building of at least fifteen major lighthouses.

The Bell Rock Lighthouse, a stone tower lighthouse 100 feet tall built in 1811, was one of Stevenson's first major achievements. Dunnet Head Lighthouse, built by Robert in 1831, is actually the northernmost point of mainland Scotland. It is located near Thurso. The views from the lighthouse are spectacular, with the Orkney Islands straight ahead.

The Mull of Galloway Lighthouse is located in southwestern Scotland at the tip of the Galloway Peninsula. It was built in 1830 with Robert Stevenson as the engineer and Brebner and Scott as the builders. It originally had an intermittent light and was one of the first lighthouses to have its walls lowered because of the strong winds they caused in the courtyards.

Three of Robert Stevenson's sons—David, Alan, and Tom—also became engineers specializing in lighthouses. The Skerryvore Lighthouse, built in 1844 by his son Alan, was even taller than Bell Rock. Noss Head, located three miles outside the town of Wick in Caithness, was built in 1849. Alan Stevenson was the engineer for the project. It sits on the easternmost projection on the northeastern coast of Scotland and is now completely automated.

The Beacon of Ornsay lies between the Isle of Skye and the mainland. It was built in 1857. David and Thomas Stevenson were the engineers for the project. It was one of the first lights to require only one keeper as a result of modern technology. It was completely automated in 1962. Its setting is one of the most beautiful in the Hebrides.

Rubh' Re Lighthouse was established in 1912 and designed by David and Charles Stevenson. The station is located on the west coast of Sutherland at the entrance of Loch Ewe near Melvaig, looking out across the Minch. It was the scene of a spectacular rescue during World War II when an American Liberty ship, the *William H. Welch,* missed

the entrance to Loch Ewe and went ashore at Black Bay. Two lightkeepers went out to the rescue across peat bogs in slush and snow, and were able to bring back fourteen survivors out of a crew of 74.

Fair Isle North Lighthouse was established in 1892, and designed by David and Charles Stevenson. The station is located on the northern end of Fair Isle in the North Sea, north of the Orkney Islands and south of the Shetland Islands. It has a range of twenty-two miles and was one of the last of the Northern Lighthouse Board's stations to be automated.

Strathy Point Lighthouse, lit in 1958, is the newest of the Northern Lighthouse Board's stations. It was the first all-electric station with a major light and fog signal. The station buildings, designed by the board's engineer, P. H. Hysolop, are laid out in a hollow square with covered passageways, giving protection from the high winds on this exposed headland.

The first lighthouse you see when you fly into Shetland is the Sumburgh Head Lighthouse on the south end of the island. It is one of the best places to spot Scotland's puffins and dolphins. Shetland's Fethaland Lighthouse was built in 1979 to act as a navigational guide to ships going in and out of the oil terminal at the Isle of Fethaland, off the northernmost tip of the Shetland Mainland. The area was once one of the biggest fishing areas in Shetland. It was designed by David A. Stevenson to be totally automatic.

In 1868, a Scotsman named Richard Henry Brunton was appointed

chief lighthouse engineer by the Japanese government at the recommendation of David and Thomas Stevenson. In this position, Brunton was responsible for founding a lighthouse service in Japan, supervising the construction of approximately fifty lighthouses around the Japanese coast, and initiating a training school and system of lighthouse keepers modeled on the Northern Lighthouse Board in Scotland. His achievement was remarkable because Japan was a closed society at the time, and this was all undertaken in just eight years. Although the construction designs and light mechanisms he used were taken from the Stevensons, he had to adapt his building techniques for a country where earthquakes were prevalent. He used stabilizing bars and in a few cases constructed an entire lighthouse in metal. He never achieved fame in Britain but is known by the Japanese as the father of Japanese lighthouses.

21

Loch Ness and Other Monsters

The oldest recorded sighting of the Loch Ness Monster was made by St. Columba. The seventh-century monk Adamnan wrote in his biography of the Christian missionary that Columba subdued the beast when it attacked his followers. The most popular version of the story credits St. Columba with raising his cross and shouting "Thou shalt go no further, nor touch this man!" The monster left and was not seen again.

The Nessie phenomenon was known only around Loch Ness and local communities until the 1933 sighting by Mrs. MacKay was reported in the local paper. Following this, the Nessie legend took off with dramatic speed. In 1941 an Italian newspaper reported that the wartime bombing of Scotland had succeeded in killing the Loch Ness Monster. Nevertheless, there are at least a dozen or more sightings of "Nessie" per year to this day. There are as many theories about the Loch Ness monster as there are sightings: a boat wakes birds swimming on the loch,

giant snakes with their heads curled, and seals that enter the loch from the sea. Another old legend tells of a ghost Viking ship that sometimes sails the loch, which is said to account for many of the head and neck sightings.

Ben MacDhui, the highest peak of the Cairngorms, claims to be home to the Cairngorm Beast, a Yeti known as the "Big Grey Man." Also famous are tales of giant snakes in Linto Hill and a three-headed giant named Red Etin who lived in Edin's fort. At least ten other lochs claim to house strange beasts.

22

Lords of Invention

Winston Churchill said, "Of all the small nations on this earth, perhaps only the Ancient Greeks surpass the Scots in their contribution to mankind." Scotland has produced some remarkable inventors, including John Logie Baird, Alexander Graham Bell, James Watt, and Charles Macintosh.

Charles Macintosh was born in Glasgow in 1766. The son of the owner of a chemical dye factory, he left school to work as a clerk, but attended scientific lectures and was a fan of the great chemist Joseph Black. Macintosh was in business for himself by the time he was twenty, taking out several patents in the use of dye materials, a new system for producing chloride of lime, used for bleaching, and even one new method for converting iron into steel. In 1823, Macintosh noticed that rubber dissolved on contact with coal-tar naptha. By applying naptha to rubber sheeting strengthened by cloth, he invented the fabric for the raincoat

that bears his name. The early models had many problems: in winter the rubber became as stiff as a board, while in summer it became somewhat sticky, seams leaked, and sometimes the rubber disintegrated. In spite of all these technical problems, the coats sold and sold.

James Watt did not actually invent the steam engine, but he took the design of two Englishmen and made it better and more useful. He applied the idea of condensation to the steam engine, and made it into something that could be used in industry.

John McAdam, born in 1756, was a surveyor and road builder. After earning a fortune in trade in New York, McAdam returned to Scotland. In doing repair and maintenance around his estate, he developed the process of "macadamization," which involved covering a road with small broken stones to form a hard surface. Richard Edgeworth, a follower of McAdam, used stone dust mixed with water to fill the gaps between the stones, thereby providing a much smoother surface. This was the forerunner of the bitumen-based binding that was to become tarmacadam. The first tarmac road to be laid was in Paris in 1854. With the development of the automobile in the early twentieth century, tarmac roads, or "black tops," came into common use.

Sir William Fairbairn, born in Kelso in 1789, developed the idea of using tubular steel, which was much stronger than solid steel, as a construction material. James Nasmyth (son of landscape artist Alexander Nasmyth) was born in Edinburgh in 1808. He started a foundry busi-

ness and became a pioneer in the design and building of steam-powered machine tools, such as the steam hammer, planing machine, pile driver, and steam lathe.

Henry Bell was born into a family of mechanics in Torphichen in Linlithgowshire. In about 1800, he began to work on a method of steam-driven propulsion in boats. Although he failed to make a successful demonstration before the admiralty, he communicated his ideas to several European countries, as well as the United States. In the United States, he was in touch with Robert Fulton and by 1807 American steamboats were successfully traveling the major waterways. In 1808, he moved to Helensburgh and by 1811 he produced his steamboat, the *Comet,* with a three horsepower engine. The *Comet,* named after the "Great Comet" of 1811, was built by Messrs. John Wood and Company at Port Glasgow. She made her trial trip on January 18, 1812 from Glasgow to Greenock, reaching five miles an hour against a headwind. In August of the same year, there are records advertising trips "to sail by the power of air, wind, and steam" upon the Clyde three times a week.

Mathematician and astronomer John Napier was born in Merchiston Castle, near Edinburgh, in 1850. Napier, who was the eighth Lord of Merchiston, studied at St. Andrews. He devised "Napier's Rod" or "Napier's Bones," an early mechanical calculation device for multiplication and division. He also developed the concept of logarithms and invented the use of the decimal point to indicate fractions.

Other famous Scottish inventors include the Reverend Patrick Bell, who invented the reaping machine that was a direct precursor of the modern combine harvester. Engineer William Murdock invented coal-gas lighting in 1792. James Beaumont Neilson (1792–1865) invented the hot blast oven, a great advance in the iron industry. His process reduced the amount of coal needed to produce iron, and greatly increased efficiency in the railway and shipbuilding industries. During the same period, engineer William Symington (1763–1831) developed the first steam-powered marine engine used to power the world's first paddle steamer.

Robert William Thomson of Stonehaven patented his vulcanized rubber pneumatic tire in 1845. It was successfully tested in London, but was rejected as being too expensive for common use. The tire was reinvented by John Dunlop in 1888. Thomson also patented the fountain pen in 1849 and a steam traction engine in 1867. Chemical engineer James Young (1811–1883) developed the process of refining oil and created the world's first oil industry based on the oil shales of West Lothian, close to Edinburgh.

Several Scots focused their engineering on connecting their nation's many islands and even connecting Scotland to England. Thomas Telford (1757–1834) , a native of Dumfriesshire, built many bridges, docks, and canals. These include the bridge over the Atlantic Ocean (the Menai Straits) linking Anglesey and Wales, Dean Bridge in Edinburgh, and the

Caledonian Canal. Sir William Arrol (1839–1913) was responsible for both the Forth Rail Bridge and the replacement Tay Rail Bridge, the two most substantial bridges in the world of their time and still in constant use today. Arrol also worked on Tower Bridge in London. Sir Robert McAlpine (1847–1934), known as "Concrete Bob," was an entrepreneur who started a large building and civil engineering firm. McAlpine was also a pioneer in the use of concrete and labor-saving machinery. He left school at the age of ten to work in a coal mine, but went on to build roads and public buildings, including Wembley Stadium in London.

The most powerful communication tool of modern times was developed and first demonstrated by John Logie Baird in 1926, when he transmitted a crude television picture from one room to another—much to the astonishment of an audience of fellow inventors. Born at Helensburgh in 1888, Baird was educated first at Glasgow Academy and then at the city's Royal Technical College before embarking upon a career of invention. Baird's inventive tendencies started at an early age when he built a crude telephone system allowing him to talk to his schoolfriends. To supply electric light for his home, he installed a gas-driven dynamo. In another experiment he caused the local electrical supply to fail after trying to make diamonds by passing a huge current through blocks of carbon. The world of electricity was not the only outlet for his inventive mind. He developed a special insulated sock that

was warm in the winter and cool in the summer, and also tried his hand at mass producing jams and chutneys.

In October 1925, he obtained the world's first real television picture and went on to demonstrate it to the British public on January 26, 1926. The picture he managed to obtain on the screen was a small thirty-line, vertically scanned, black and red image. Following that first momentous transmission in 1926, Baird succeeded in sending a picture by telephone wire from London to Glasgow in 1927, surpassing this with a transatlantic transmission in 1928. In 1929, Baird's television company provided the pictures for the first ever public broadcast by the BBC, and broadcast the first high-definition color picture in 1937. Unfortunately for Baird, his rivals soon pioneered systems that surpassed his. He also took out a patent on fiber optics, a technology now used to carry many telephone calls and traffic on the Internet. His most famous invention—the television—assured his place in history as the person who changed the way we see the world forever.

23

Lost and Found

Infamous pirate William "Captain" Kidd was born in Greenock (Inverclyde) in 1645. The son of a clergyman, Kidd ran a small merchant fleet from New York. He fought as a privateer to protect Anglo-American trade routes in the West Indies from the French and in 1691 was rewarded by New York City. He was then employed by the British Navy, based in Madagascar, to stamp out piracy in the Indian Ocean, but instead became a pirate himself. He captured the Armenian ship *Quedah Merchant,* with cargo rumored to be worth more than $100,000 dollars. He eventually surrendered in Boston in 1699, and was transported to London, where he was tried and hanged on Execution Dock on the River Thames in 1701. Much of his treasure has never been recovered.

Although it belongs to Trinity College in Dublin, The Book of Kells, one of the finest illuminated manuscripts to have survived from the

Celtic period, is thought to have been started and possibly completed at Iona Abbey.

The "Lost Clan" is the name given to the descendants of the elite Scottish guard that once served the French monarchy. In 1525, members of this guard were caught in blizzards while crossing the Alps and decided to settle there. It is believed that descendants of the Lost Clan still inhabit the area.

There has been speculation that the Stone of Destiny, now in Edinburgh Castle, is not the original artifact. History has it that the original was carved not as a plain sandstone block, and that monks fooled King Edward I when he stole the stone in 1296. In 1950, the Stone of Destiny was stolen from Westminster Abbey and hidden in Arbroath.

In 2002, a garment believed to have been worn by a Sioux warrior killed in the 1890 Wounded Knee massacre was returned to its native land from Scotland. The relic was displayed for more than a century in the Kelvingrove Art Gallery in Glasgow after George Crager, a member of Buffalo Bill's Wild West Show, gave it to the museum in 1891. The shirt remained on display until John Earl, of Cherokee descent, visited the Home of the Brave exhibition in the McLellan Galleries in Glasgow in 1992. "I immediately knew from my own heart that it shouldn't be there." The Glasgow City Council agreed to repatriate the shirt and it was officially handed back to descendants of the battle victims at a special ceremony in South Dakota. A total of twenty-nine descendants of

the victims stood around the mass grave in the state capital of Pierre as Zack Bear Shield offered prayers at the ceremony. The shirt was unfolded to the sound of bagpipes. Bullet holes could be seen on the left side of the fringed cloth. The shirt will be displayed at the Cultural Heritage Center in Pierre, South Dakota, until the Lakota, one of the seven Sioux tribes, can build their own museum near Wounded Knee.

24

Music and Dance

When you think of Scottish music, bagpipes may be the first thing to cross your mind, but Scottish folk musicians were also wonderful pipers, fiddlers, and accordianists, and were especially adept at the tin whistle and the moothie (mouth organ or harmonica).

When one of Scotland's most famous traditional musicians, Jimmy Shand, died at the age of ninety-two in December 2000, it was the loss of a national treasure. The former miner from Fife recorded hundreds of songs on accordian from 1933 up until the 1990s. Millions of people around the world danced to the music of Shand. Shands's first musical instrument was the moothie, before his father, himself a skilled melodian player, taught him to play the instrument. When Shand was fourteen and left school to work in the mineshafts, he played his melodian in the evenings and on the weekends, even playing at social events, weddings, and competitions. In his mid-twenties, Jimmy began to work in a

music shop in Dundee and switched to the chromatic button-key accordion.

Willie Kemp was born in 1889 in Oldmeldrum, Aberdeenshire and first performed publicly at his parents' hotel. When radio arrived in the 1920s, Kemp quickly became popular, and like others of his generation went on to a successful recording career. In addition to composing and singing ballads, he played tin whistle, trump, and ocarina. He recorded many songs and tunes with accordionist Curley MacKay.

The whistle is a simple member of the flute family that has been played for centuries. Bone whistle-like instruments have been found from 180,000 years ago; more recent bone flutes have been found in Dublin from the twelfth century, and the Tusculum whistle in the Museum of Scotland, made of brass or bronze, was found with pottery dating from the fourteenth and fifteenth centuries. (The "Tusculum whistle," excavated in North Berwick in 1907, is little more than five inches long and has six finger holes.) Other whistles have been made from clay, wood, and reeds, but the principle for making the whistle sound is always the same: A narrow gap is created in a mouthpiece through which air is blown, and holes in the barrel are stopped or opened to vary the pitch.

Principally seen as a rustic toy associated with shepherds and bucolic idylls, the whistle was generally not taken seriously in Scotland by dance masters, music teachers, and publishers. Wee Willie White was a

nineteenth-century musician in Glasgow who played the whistle. So was Carl Volti (born Archie Milligan in 1849), who became well known as a composer of classical music and fiddle tunes in his youth.

In the 1840s, Englishman Robert Clarke invented the Clarke Pennywhistle, made from bending tin into a tube shape, and its mass production in the years to follow ensured its popularity. Photographs of Aberdeenshire bothy bands from the late-nineteenth century show whistle players posing along with melodians, fiddles, pipes, and chanters. The rise in popularity of Irish music in the 1960s and 1970s, and its popularity ever since, has led to an upsurge of people learning the whistle, and more and more types have been made. The tin whistle today is mostly associated with Irish music, and many people taking up the whistle in Scotland are aiming to play Irish music in Irish styles.

Fiddle music is very popular, especially in Shetland where Tom Anderson and Aly Bain were among the most famous fiddlers. Orkney also has a long history of fiddle music, though not as well known. James Barnett, a fiddler from Kirkwall, was born in 1847. The tune *The New Brig o' Dee* is attributed to him. Another Kirkwall fiddler was Peter Lennie, and Jimmy Johnstone from Deerness composed several tunes as well. David Eunson of Colster was a fiddler and fiddle maker. His cousin, David Horne, known as Cubbie Roo, toured Australia with his Scottish Dance Band. Concerned that public interest in Scottish fiddle

music was waning, James Stewart Robertson set about compiling an encyclopedia of Scottish dance music in 1884.

Contemporary Scottish music groups focus on Scottish music from all periods. One of the best known is the Whistlebinkies. Formed during the great surge of interest in traditional and Celtic music and song in the late 1960s, the group led the revival in the use of the bellows-blown bagpipes in Scotland and were the first to combine the three national instruments—the fiddle, bagpipes, and clarsach (a small Scottish harp)—in regular performance. The Whistlebinkies use authentic traditional instruments and their repertory is drawn from all periods of Scottish music and from all regions of the country. They have toured extensively, taking Scottish music to France, Germany, Italy, Finland, Iceland, Taiwan, Estonia, and all the Celtic countries. In 1991, they were the first Scottish music group to tour the Peoples Republic of China. Recent festival appearances include the Edinburgh International Festival, the Edinburgh Festival Fringe, Glasgow Mayfest, the Hong Kong Folk Festival, and the Festival Interceltique at Lorient, Brittany.

Jock Tamson's Bairns is one of Scotland's most respected bands, carrying the torch for true Scottish music since their inception at the end of the 1970s. Their *Lasses Fashion* album of the 1980s is still regarded as one of the finest expressions of Scottish traditional music. The Bairns have been involved in other influential groups—as members of Ossian, Easy Club, Ceolbeg, Cauld Blast Orchestra, The Ghillies, and

others—and in dance bands such as The Occasionals and Bella McNabs. They have also appeared in Scottish theater and on radio and TV.

The earliest types of Scottish dances were ring dances. There are several references in early fifteenth-century literature to dancing in rings. There are also some references to carols, which in this context means dance and song combined. Dancing at feasts is mentioned as early as 1375.

The next forms of dancing that appeared in the literature were "courtly" dances. These dances were performed in many of the courts of Europe—pavans, galliards, rounds, and bransles, among others. There are references to these in the sixteenth century, as well as to Morris dancing and the reel. The word "reel" has two meanings in dancing. One meaning is a figure-of-eight movement. The other meaning is a dance that has the reel figure as a prominent part. The threesome reel probably dates back to the end of the sixteenth century. Dancing competitions are mentioned as early as the late sixteenth century.

The 1700s saw the full formation and formal instructions for Scottish country dancing, which flourished throughout the drawing rooms and ballrooms of the 1700s and the first part of the 1800s. By the middle of the nineteenth century, country dancing was losing popularity. At the beginning of the twentieth century, the Scottish Country Dance Society was formed. This group "standardized" the dances, prob-

ably at some loss to regional variations and historical accuracy, but they revived Scottish country dancing, which remains popular today.

Scottish Highland dancing is one of the oldest forms of folk dance, and both modern ballet and square dancing can trace their roots back to the Highlands. Dating back to the eleventh or twelfth century, the Highland dances of Scotland tended to be highly athletic male celebratory dances of triumph in war, performed over swords and spiked shields. According to tradition, the old kings and chiefs of Scotland used the Highland Games as a way of choosing the best men for their retinue and men at arms. Highland dancing was one of the many ways men were tested for strength, stamina, accuracy, and agility. The Scottish military regiments used Highland dancing as a form of training to develop stamina and agility, but this has become less common these days. Competitive Highland dancing started during the Highland revival of Victorian Britain, and was for men only. Women began competing only at the turn of the century. Over time, the dancing style has become more refined and now shares many elements of classical ballet. Although historically Highland dancing was restricted to men, today it is mostly performed by women. No matter who dances them, Highland dances require both athletic and artistic skill.

The Highland Fling is danced on the spot, and is said to be based on the antics of a stag on a hillside; the grouped fingers and upheld arms

represent the antlers. The term *ceilidh,* used now to mean an evening of traditional dance, usually with live music, translates literally from Gaelic as "visit" and was once used more generally to mean a social gathering.

Scottish country dancing today involves groups of six to ten people (most of the time) of mixed sex (most of the time). A "set" of dancing to the music of reels, jigs, and strathspeys played on the fiddle, accordion, flute, piano, and drums (no bagpipes), the dance often combines solo figures for the "first couple" in the set with movements for all the dancers. There are over seven thousand different dances catalogued, of which maybe one thousand or so are of lasting importance. Many of these dances derive from traditional sources such as old manuscripts and printed dance collections, but many others have been devised in the fairly recent past (the last fifty years or so). This fusion of the traditional and the modern—as well as its ongoing evolution—are part of the attraction of Scottish country dancing, which is very popular in both the United States and Canada. There are groups and organizations in many large cities.

Among modern musicians, Scotland lays claim to Patrick Doyle, a graduate of the Royal Scottish Academy of Music and Drama. After a successful career acting and writing music for television (he even had a small role in *Chariots of Fire),* he joined Kenneth Branagh's Renaissance

Theatre Company in 1987, where he began to write scores for theater and film. He wrote the music for Kenneth Branagh's first feature film in 1989, *Henry V,* and has written the scores for *Dead Again*, *Much Ado About Nothing, Carlito's Way,* and *Sense and Sensibility,* as well as *Bridget Jones's Diary* and Robert Altman's *Gosford Park.*

25

Poets

The most famous Scottish poet is, of course, Robert Burns, the eighteenth-century poet considered Scotland's national poet. Among many other works he wrote *"Auld Lang Syne"* which is now sung worldwide at the end of functions and particularly at the end of the year. The Scots celebrate "Burns's Night" on his birthday, January 25, with dinners held in his honor. He rates his own listing as one of the 101 sources of Scottish pride.

One of England's greatest poets, George Gordon Noel Byron, was born in London but spent his formative years in Scotland. He was among the most famous of the English Romantic poets; his contemporaries included Percy Shelley and John Keats. As a child, he was known simply as George Gordon. Born with a clubfoot, Byron was extremely sensitive of his lameness. He was taken by his mother, Catherine Gordon, to Aberdeen, where he lived in lodgings on a meager income and at-

tended the local grammar school. He was also a satirist whose poetry and personality captured the imagination of Europe. His major works include *Childe Harold's Pilgrimage* (1812–18) and *Don Juan* (1819–24).

James "Ossian" MacPherson, a Celtic and Highland poet, influenced the European Romantic movement. Other famous Scottish poets include Barbour, Dunmbar, Heninson, Lyndsay, and Helen Cruickshank. English poets William and Dorothy Wordsworth spent much time visiting Scotland and it inspired many of their works.

Norman MacCaig, born in 1910, is regarded as the greatest Scottish poet of his generation. He was awarded the Queen's Gold Medal for poetry in 1986. He was a close friend of Hugh MacDiarmid (1892–1978), poet, socialist, and a founder of the Scottish National Party. His best-known work is perhaps "A Drunk Man Looks at the Thistle." MacDiarmid was actually a pen name; his real name was Christopher Murry Grieve.

26

Puffins

The puffin is a comical-looking bird with black and white plumage—much like a penguin—and a huge multicolored bill. It has a whirring flight and is an excellent swimmer and diver, using its wings to propel itself through water and using its large red feet as rudders. There is a famous colony of puffins on the island of Fidra. Puffins, often referred to as the seabird clowns of the air, gather in usually inaccessible offshore island puffinries to breed. They spend the winter in the North Sea and North Atlantic before returning to the islands in the spring. Although dates vary slightly from year to year, the first puffins start to return in early April. Puffin numbers increase until mid-July, when they are at their peak with all the nonbreeders and juveniles present. At that time, the air is alive with parents returning with mouthfuls of sandeel, making a dash for the safety of the burrow before the herring gulls can mob them.

Puffins nest in burrows underground, under boulders, or in rocky crevices. Mothers lay one egg, which hatches about six weeks later. After hatching, the young puffin remains underground, concealed in the nest until the night comes, when it heads for the open sea, not to return until it is ready to breed, usually some five years later. By late August, all the puffins will be gone, the youngsters going to sea under cover of darkness, leaving the islands to the seals and the winter storms.

Puffins are skillful fishermen, able to catch and hold up to a dozen or so sandeel in their beaks. Puffins favor grassy slopes, covered in pink thrift and other wildflowers, the perfect backdrop for photographers keen to capture the social gatherings and huge wheeling flybys, that are so characteristic of a puffin colony.

In 1955, there were only seven pairs of Atlantic puffins recorded on the Isle of May. At the latest count, there were over 100,000. The islands of Fidra and Craigleith are also home to large puffin colonies.

27

The Royal Scots

The Royal Scots, the oldest infantry regiment in the British Army, was formed in 1633 when Sir John Hepburn, under a royal warrant granted by King Charles I, raised a body of men in Scotland for service in France. By 1635, he commanded a force of over eight thousand, including many who had fought as mercenaries in the "Green Brigade" for King Gustavus Adolphus of Sweden. It was by virtue of the royal warrant that the entire regiment was considered British; a regular force in a standing army that could be recalled to Britain at will. In 1661, the Regiment was summoned to Britain to bridge the gap between the disbandment of the New Model Army and the creation of a regular army, organized along the same lines as the British units in foreign service. The regiment was thus the original model for all others.

In 1680, the regiment was sent to Tangiers and won its first battle honor. On its return to England in 1684, Charles II conferred on them

the title "The Royal Regiment of Foot." During Monmouth's rebellion in 1685, five companies formed part of the force concentrated against the rebels, who they met at Sedgemoor. The following year, the regiment was divided into two battalions and was not to have less than that many until 1949.

The Royal Scots saw service under Malborough during the War of the Spanish Succession and followed this with garrison duty in Ireland, where they remained until 1742. From this date forward, the two battalions were usually separated and posted far apart. The First Battalion moved in 1743 to Germany to take part in the War of Austrian Succession, and was involved in the Battle of Fontenoy. In the following year, the Second Battalion joined in the fight against the Young Pretender, culminating in the Battle of Culloden. In 1751, the army was numbered and thereafter the regiment was officially designated the First or Royal Regiment of Foot. The War of Austrian Succession had not settled the chief issue between Britain and France—colonial supremacy. In both India and America the fighting continued, and most of the regiment's active service in the thirty-five years that followed was in the New World. During the Seven Years War, the Second Battalion found itself involved in many actions, including the capture of Montreal in 1760 and Havana in 1762. Then, after a period of service at home and in the Mediterranean, it was the First Battalion's turn for service in the West Indies. There disease rather than the enemy accounted for most deaths;

between 1793 and 1796 the British lost forty thousand men in the West Indies. The Royals lost five officers and four hundred men, well over half the battalion strength.

During the Napoleonic Wars, the regiment was increased to four battalions. The First Battalion spent the entire war in the Americas. The Second Battalion took part in the capture of Egypt (1801), then moved to the West Indies (1803–05) before travelling to India, the first time that any part of the regiment had been there. They were to stay until 1831. In contrast, the Third and Fourth Battalions remained in Europe. The Fourth Battalion stayed on home service, supplying drafts for the other three battalions until 1812. The Third Battalion first saw action at Corunna in 1808 and then took part in the Peninsular War. Then came the battles of Quatre Bras and Waterloo, which cost the battalion 363 casualties out of a strength of 624. In 1817, it was disbanded, the fourth battalion having suffered a similar fate the previous year.

The next ninety years produced a considerable number of moves for both remaining battalions. They served in India in 1817–31, the Crimean War, and the Boer War. In World War I the number of battalions of Royal Scots increased to more than 100,000 men, of whom 11,000 were killed and over 40,000 wounded.

At the start of World War II, the First Battalion embarked for France but was forced into a retreat that ended at Dunkirk. Royal Scots were also based in Hong Kong, Burma, Italy, and Palestine. Since 1945,

the regiment has continued to serve in many parts of the world, including Germany, Korea, Cyprus, Suez, Aden, and Ireland. In 1983, the regiment celebrated its 350th Anniversary. In December 1990, the Royal Scots took part in the Gulf War. The Regimental Headquarters and Museum of the Royal Scots are at Edinburgh Castle.

28

Royalty

Kenneth MacAlpin is widely believed to be the ruler who united the Scots and Picts and became King of Scotland (as we know it) in 843 A.D. Lord MacBeth (c.1005–1057), grandson of Malcolm II, was the last of Scotland's Gaelic Kings. Although best known as a villain in William Shakespeare's *Macbeth,* in reality he was a good king for Scotland.

Stuart (spelled Stewart in England) was the Royal House of Scotland between 1371 and 1603 and, following the Union of the Crowns, of Scotland and England between 1603 and 1714. There were fourteen Stuart monarchs in all. The line is descended from Walter, appointed Great Steward of Scotland by King David I (1084–1153). Another Walter, the sixth Great Steward, distinguished himself at Bannockburn and was knighted by Robert the Bruce. He also supported Paisley Abbey. Walter married Robert's sister, and their son later became King Robert II.

A branch of this family forms the Stuarts of Bute, who are heredi-

tary sheriffs of Bute and Arran, keepers of Rothesay Castle, and marquesses of Bute. The Stuarts of Darnley became the Earls of Lennox. The family can trace its ancestry back to Brittany (France), and had lands in East Lothian and Renfrewshire.

Mary, Queen of Scots (1542–1587) was the last Roman Catholic monarch of Scotland. Although remembered as a heroic figure, she was a poor ruler, lacking the political acumen of her cousin, Queen Elizabeth I of England. After religious disputes with John Knox and political intrigue involving her nobles, she was imprisoned and forced to abdicate in 1567 in favor of her son, James VI. She was eventually executed in 1587 for treason. In 1603, James VI succeeded Elizabeth I as James I of England, Scotland, and Ireland. In 1633, Charles I, son of James VI, was crowned King of Scotland. In 1649, England was declared a commonwealth, ending the line of Scottish royalty.

Charles Edward Stewart (Bonnie Prince Charlie) tried to regain the English throne. The "Young Pretender" was the grandson of James VII of Scotland (James II of England), who was exiled by William of Orange. The French-backed Jacobite Rebellion of 1745 was intended to restore him to the throne, but ended in disarray and bloody defeat at Culloden in 1746. He escaped to France with the help of the Hebridian Flora MacDonald, and lived comfortably in exile. He died, a despondent drunk, in 1788, and is buried in St. Peter's, Rome.

29

Scientists

Think the Scots haven't made any special scientific contributions to the world? Let's not forget that Dolly, the world's first cloned sheep, was born in Edinburgh in 1995. So was Sir Alexander Fleming, whose discovery of penicillin changed the nature of recovery from disease. Born in Ayrshire in 1881, he discovered the world's first antibiotic drug as a result of a laboratory "accident" involving mold that had grown on a bacterial culture. Fleming was knighted and received the Nobel Prize in 1944.

Mathematician and physicist William Thomson (Lord Kelvin of Largs) was born in Belfast, Ireland in 1824 but was brought up in Scotland. Kelvin's life became inextricably bound up with Glasgow and its university. He matriculated at the age of eleven to study at Glasgow University, where his father was a professor of mathematics. After a period of study at Cambridge, Kelvin returned to Glasgow in 1846, becoming professor

of natural philosophy (physics). His name lives on, particularly in the science of thermodynamics, where he proposed an absolute scale of temperature. A Kelvin degree is equivalent to a Celsius degree, but the scale is adjusted so that zero represents absolute zero, the temperature at which all molecular motion ceases. On this scale, water freezes at about 273K, and boils at about 373K.

Kelvin was also extremely active as a practical scientist, making developments in electric telegraphy and inventing other useful devices. In 1866, he supervised the laying of a marine cable from Ireland to Newfoundland. He was knighted in 1874 for his services to telegraphy. A keen sailor, he invented several instruments useful for navigation, including an improved compass, a sounding machine, and a tide predictor. In all, he published well over six hundred scientific papers, starting at the age of fifteen.

James Gregory was born in November of 1638, at Drumoak, Aberdeen, into the talented Gregory family, whose members included a host of doctors and physicians. The Gregory family produced mathematicians and doctors for centuries, somewhat akin to the Bach family's line of musicians. Educated at Marischal College in Aberdeen, Gregory published the first proof of the fundamental theorem of calculus. In 1663, he published *Optica Promota* (The Advance of Optics), in which he described the first practical reflecting telescope, now called the Gregorian

telescope. He also introduced the estimation of stellar distances by photometric means.

In about 1665 he went to Padua to study mathematics, writing *Vera Circuli et Hyperbolae Quadratura* (The True Squaring of the Circle and of the Hyperbola) in 1667. In this work he showed the distinction between convergent and divergent series. He also wrote *Geometriae Pars Universalis* (The Universal Part of Geometry) in 1668, which defined a series of rules for finding the areas of curves and the volumes of their solids of revolution.

Gregory was professor of mathematics at St. Andrews University (1669–74) and Edinburgh University (1674–75). He is believed to have been a great influence on Isaac Newton, and was certainly the main link between Scotland and Newton's work, whose mathematics were being taught in Scottish universities before they were taught in Oxford or Cambridge. Gregory died in Edinburgh at the age of thirty-seven with less recognition than he deserved, in October of 1675.

Chemist Joseph Black (1728–1799) was professor of anatomy and chemistry at Glasgow University (1756) and professor of medicine and chemistry at Edinburgh University (1766). He developed the concept of latent heat and discovered carbon dioxide (fixed air). Black is considered the father of quantitative chemistry.

Sir David Brewster, born in 1781, was a physicist and principal of St.

Andrews (1838) and Edinburgh Universities (1859), where he worked with polarized light. He invented the kaleidoscope and suggested it might be useful for designing carpets.

Geologist and geographer Sir Roderick Impey Murchison was born in Tarradale in Rothshire in 1792. He was responsible for discovering and naming the Silurian geological system, and with one of his companions, Adam Sedgwick, the Devonian system. Murchison led expeditions to the Russian Empire from 1840 to 1845. He was a founder of the Royal Geological Society of London and its president for many years. He was knighted in 1846, and the Murchison Falls (in Uganda) and the Murchison River (in Australia) are named after him.

Geologist Sir Archibald Geikie, who specialized in volcanic geology and microscopic examination of rocks, was professor of geology at the University of Edinburgh between 1870 and 1881, and then Director General of the U.K. Geological Survey until 1901. His brother, James Geikie, was noted for his contribution to mapping the geology of Scotland and wrote the standard work of the day on the glacial period. He succeeded his brother as professor of geology at the University of Edinburgh, a post that he held until 1914.

Botanist Robert Brown was born in Montrose in 1773. The son of a clergyman, he studied medicine at the Universities of Aberdeen and Edinburgh. While visiting London in 1798, he came to the attention of Sir Joseph Banks. On Banks's recommendation Brown became natural-

ist to the survey of Australia (1801–05) led by Matthew Flinders, and brought back a collection of nearly 4,000 new plant species. He was the first to recognize the difference between the coniferous plants (gymnosperms) and the flowering plants (angiosperms). Banks again took an interest in Brown's career, making him librarian and curator of his extensive natural history collection. On Banks's death, Brown transferred this collection to the British Museum, becoming its first Keeper of Botany. Brown made his most significant contribution in the classification of plants. He observed what became known as Brownian Motion the movement of fine particles in a liquid (1827), while examining pollen grains in water. In addition, while studying orchids, he first described the nucleus in plant cells and realized that this structure was fundamental to their reproduction.

Sir Thomas Makdougall Brisbane was a soldier and an astronomer, born in Largs, Ayrshire in 1773. As Governor-General of the Australian state of New South Wales, he set up an observatory and cataloged more than seven thousand stars. The city of Brisbane (in Australia) is named after him.

Many Scottish chemists were responsible for the discovery of elements. Sir William Ramsay, born in Glasgow in 1852, discovered argon with Lord Rayleigh in 1894. In 1895, Ramsay produced helium and, in 1898, in cooperation with Morris Travers, he identified neon, krypton, and xenon. In 1903, with Frederick Soddy, he noted the transmutation

of radium into helium, which led to the discovery of the density and relative atomic mass of radium. He was knighted in 1902 and received the Nobel Prize in 1904. Alexander Crum Brown, an organic chemist, was born in Edinburgh. He studied in London and Leipzig before returning to Edinburgh in 1863, where he held the chair of chemistry that now bears his name. He devised the system of representing chemical compounds in diagrammatic form, with connecting lines representing bonds. Thomas Graham, born in Glasgow in 1805 and educated at Glasgow University, formulated "Graham's Law" on the diffusion of gases. He is referred to as the father of colloid chemistry.

Oceanographer and explorer William Spiers Bruce studied medicine at Edinburgh University, and became one of the first of his era to explore the Antarctic in 1892. He was leader of the Scottish National Antarctic Expedition that discovered Coats Land in 1902–04, and founded the Scottish Oceanographical Laboratory in Edinburgh in 1907.

Sir Hugh Dalrymple (Lord Drummore) invented hollow-pipe drainage and Sir James Dewar, physicist and chemist, born in Kincardine, Fife, in 1842, invented the vacuum flask. James Clerk Maxwell (1831–1879) was a mathematician and physicist who contributed significantly to the study of electromagnetism and paved the way for the study of quantum physics. He is ranked along with Newton and Einstein as one of the world's greatest physicists.

Scots have made enormous contributions to medicine as well. Alexander Monro, born in 1697, was professor of anatomy at the University of Edinburgh. He founded the Edinburgh Royal Infirmary and established Edinburgh as a major center of medical teaching and research. Alexander Monro the Second succeeded his father as professor of anatomy in Edinburgh. He discovered the lymphatic systems, mapped the structure and function of the nervous system, and noted the physiological effects of drugs.

Army surgeon George Cleghorn discovered that quinine bark could be used to cure malaria, a form of which was endemic in Britain in the eighteenth century. Sir Patrick Manson, born in 1844 in Old Meldrum, Aberdeenshire, was a pioneer of tropical medicine, developing it as a distinct field of study. He showed that malaria was carried by mosquitoes, and also did valuable research on sleeping sickness and beri-beri.

Sir James Young Simpson (1811–1870), obstetrician, and son of a baker, pioneered the use of anesthetics, particularly chloroform, developing its use in surgery and midwifery. He championed its use against medical and religious opposition. Queen Victoria used chloroform during childbirth, and this brought general acceptance. He also pioneered obstetric techniques and was responsible for many hospital practice reforms.

Elsie Inglis, born in 1864, was a leading surgeon and suffragette. She improved maternity facilities and fought for better health care for

women in Scotland. She set up a maternity hospital in Edinburgh staffed only by women. During the First World War, she set up hospitals for the troops in Serbia and Russia.

Joseph Lister was an English surgeon who was a professor at Glasgow and Edinburgh Universities. Influenced by Louis Pasteur, he pioneered the use of antiseptics. In 1867, he announced that his patients at Glasgow Royal Infirmary had remained clear of infection for nine months. His work dramatically reduced the number of postopertive deaths due to infection.

At the same time, Sir Henry Duncan Littlejohn (1826–1914), born in Edinburgh in 1826 and a graduate of the University of Edinburgh, was doing pioneering work in medicine and health. As Edinburgh's first medical officer of health in 1862, he improved sanitation and instituted the legal requirement to register occurrences of infectious diseases, allowing the authorities to act to prevent epidemics.

30

Scotch Tape and Other Misnomers

Scotch tape was neither invented in Scotland nor by a Scotsman. It was invented in 1930 by an engineer at Minnesota Mining (3M) named Richard G. Drew. It was the world's first transparent cellophane adhesive tape. Drew also invented the first masking tape in 1925, a two-inch-wide tan paper tape. The first tape dispenser was invented in 1935.

The term "Scot free," comes from an early municipal tax called scot, which came from an old Norse word, *skot,* rather than any form of Scottish word. If you did not have to pay the tax you were "scot-free," and sometimes poor people got away scot-free. In modern usage it is often used as "scot-free," meaning exempt from payment or punishment.

The exclamation "Great Scott" originated in America and refers to General Winfield Scott (1786–1866), probably due to his notorious fussiness and pomposity when he was a candidate for president of the United States.

To scotch a rumor is to expose it. In this case, scotch has nothing to do with Scotland, but rather the old French word *escocher*—to cut. Speaking of cutting, to scotch a piece of meat or fish means to score it with the tip of a knife—nothing to do with Scotland but maybe, once again, the French *escocher.*

A recipe for Scotch chicken came from *The Whole Duty of a Woman* (1737), whose compiler took it from Charles Carter (1732). There is no recipe like it in *Mrs. McLintock's Receipts for Cookery and Pastry-Work* (1736), the first cookbook to be published in Scotland, although she does have an interesting recipe for Chicken Pye that includes gooseberries and sounds like a regional dish.

A Scotch pill was a physic made with aloes, jalap, gamboge, and anise. Overuse was said to be fatal.

The Scotch game is one of the simplest of all chess openings. Its main idea is an attack on the center using rapid and aggressive moves. The name derives from its successful use in correspondence games between the London Chess Club and the Edinburgh Chess Club in the period between 1824 and 1848. Less popular after the 1850's, it was unseen in world championships for a century until resurrected by Kasparov and Karpov in 1990. The Scotch gambit is a variation of the Scotch game where a violent attack on the center is aided by the gambit of a pawn sacrifice.

Scotland Yard received its name when the task of organizing and

designing the "New Police" was placed in the hands of Colonel Charles Rowan and Richard Mayne. The two commissioners occupied a private house at 4 Whitehall Place, the back of which opened onto a courtyard. Number 4 Whitehall Place backed onto a court called Great Scotland Yard, one of three streets incorporating the words "Scotland Yard" in their names. The street names supposedly derived from the land being owned by a man called Scott during the Middle Ages. The back premises of 4 Whitehall Place was used as a police station. It was this address that led to the headquarters of the Metropolitan Police being known as Scotland Yard. Another story about the use of Scotland Yard as the police headquarters credits the name to the fact that the site had been a residence owned by the kings of Scotland, used by them and their ambassadors when staying in London. The residence became known as "Scotland." The courtyard was later used by Sir Christopher Wren and known as "Scotland Yard."

31

Scots in American History

Scots appear to have been among the earliest European travelers to America. The Norse saga of Leif Eriksson recounts that on a voyage to what is now assumed to be North America around the year 1000 A.D., two Scots who had emigrated to Scandinavia were the first to be sent ashore to explore the New World.

One of the first Scottish settlements in America was established in South Carolina in 1684 for Presbyterian dissidents. Many Scottish immigrants of the seventeenth century were deported as criminals or because they were Covenanters, people who refused to accept anything less than complete religious freedom. Thousands of Scots emigrated to Virginia and the Carolinas. They then tamed the Kentucky and Tennessee wilderness and headed farther west.

In the late-eighteenth and early-nineteenth centuries, the Highland chiefs found they couldn't make any money from their lands with the

clan system no longer in place (it was a subsistence system anyway). So, they leased their lands to the sheep farmers and the tenants had to go. Some of the people were forced to move to unproductive lands near the sea to participate in the extremely lucrative kelp farming business (a residue was used in military manufactures during the Napoleonic Wars). When the bottom fell out of this market after 1815, more farmers had to go. This process continued for about twenty-five to fifty years and is known as the Highland Clearances.

The years 1763 through 1775 saw a huge influx of Scottish refugees from the Highlands—the result of the harsh measures taken against them following the Jacobite defeat at Culloden in 1746.

Many of the early American patriots were Scottish or of Scottish descent. James Craik, a Scot from Dumfriesshire, was a physician and surgeon in the American revolutionary army, and a close friend of President George Washington. Patrick Henry, leader of the political agitation that contributed to the American Revolution, was a member of the Continental Congress and the greatest orator of his generation. His father was Scottish.

In grade school we all heard of the escapades of John Paul Jones leading the colonies' navy during the American Revolution, but did the teachers happen to mention that he was Scottish? John Paul was born at Arbigland, Kirkbean, Kirkcudbright in 1747. Apprenticed to a merchant at age thirteen, he went to sea and seven years later received his first com-

mand. After several successful years as a merchant skipper in the West Indies trade, John Paul immigrated to the British colonies in North America and there added "Jones" to his name. At the outbreak of the American Revolution, Jones was in Virginia. He cast his lot with the rebels, and in December 1775, he was commissioned first lieutenant in the Continental Navy, serving aboard the flagship *Alfred.* On November 1, 1777, he commanded the *Ranger,* sailing for France. Sailing into Quiberon Bay, France, in February 1778, Jones and Admiral La Motte Piquet exchanged gun salutes—the first time that the Stars and Stripes, the flag of the new nation, was officially recognized by a foreign government.

Early in 1779, the French king gave Jones an old East Indian vessel, which he refitted, repaired, and renamed *Bon Homme Richard* as a compliment to his patron, Benjamin Franklin. Commanding four other ships and two French privateers, he sailed out to raid English ships. On September 23, 1779, his ship engaged the *HMS Serapis* in the North Sea off Famborough Head, England. *Richard* was blasted in the initial exchange, losing much of her firepower and many of her gunners. Captain Richard Pearson, commander of the *Serapis,* called out to Jones, asking if he surrendered. Jones's reply: "I have not yet begun to fight!" It was a bloody battle and although the *Bon Homme Richard* began to sink, Jones's seamen won the battle. After the American Revolution, Jones

served as a rear admiral in the service of Empress Catherine of Russia, but returned to Paris in 1790.

Even in the colonial period before the revolution, Scotsmen held important positions in America. James Alexander left Edinburgh in 1695 and rose to become attorney general of Pennsylvania. In 1735, he defended a printer named Zenger on charges of libel against the royal governor. Zenger had accused the governor of rigging elections and this was considered a libel against the king himself. Alexander persuaded the jury to vote for an acquittal, thus pioneering freedom of the press and free speech. He was disbarred for defending Zenger. Along with Benjamin Franklin, he was one of the founders of the American Philosophical Society.

Clergyman John Witherspoon was born in 1723 in Gifford, East Lothian. He was minister at Beith, then Paisley, and came to America in 1768 to become president of Princeton University (then the College of New Jersey). Witherspoon taught and influenced many future American leaders, and helped frame the Declaration of Independence, which he later signed. He also brought the beliefs of the Scottish Enlightenment to America and was influential in establishing the doctrine of separation of church and state.

Robert Dinwiddie (1693–1770) was born near Glasgow and was the lieutenant governor of Virginia. He insisted that the colonies should

raise money for their own protection. He discovered George Washington's talents and sent him to resist the French. Thus he was an important figure in American History and has been called the "Grandfather of the United States."

Nine out of thirteen governers of the newly created United States of America were Scots. Alexander Hamilton, whose father was Scottish, was one of the authors of the *Federalist Essays*, which influenced the formation of the United States Constitution. He became America's first secretary of the treasury. General Henry Knox, a Scottish-American, was the first secretary of war.

Thomas Jefferson, the third president of the United States, was of Scots descent and one of the most brilliant individuals in history. His interests were boundless, and his accomplishments great and varied. He was a philosopher, educator, naturalist, politician, scientist, architect, inventor, pioneer in scientific farming, musician, and writer, and he was the foremost spokesman for democracy of his day. He was a direct descendant of Thomas Randolph, signer of the Declaration of Arbroath and nephew of Robert de Bruce. As president, Jefferson strengthened the powers of the executive branch of government. He was the first president to lead a political party, and through it he exercised control over Congress. He had great faith in popular rule, and it is this optimism that is the essence of what came to be called "Jeffersonian democracy."

Saint Elizabeth Ann Bayley Seton founded Sisters of Charity in Baltimore in 1809. David Douglas (1798–1834) was an adventurous botanist. Born in Scone (Perthshire), he discovered more than two hundred new plant species in North America, including the Douglas fir. He died from injuries he received after falling into a bull pit in Hawaii. General Winfield Scott, a Scottish-American, commanded American forces during the Mexican War of 1846–48. His grandfather fought at the Battle of Culloden.

The trickle of emigrants leaving Scotland became a flood from the middle of the nineteenth century until the third decade of the twentieth century. It is estimated that over 44 million emigrants left Europe between 1821 and 1915, and more than 2 million of them were Scots. The popular image of the emigrant Scot is that of a refugee from the Highland Clearances, and in the first half of nineteenth century emigrants from the Highlands and islands made up a disproportionate amount of the total number of people leaving Scotland. However, there were many reasons for emigration, and emigrants came from all areas of Scotland. In the later nineteenth century, emigration to America was predominantly from towns, while Canada, Australia, and New Zealand attracted tenant farmers and farm servants. Although poverty and land hunger accounted for a high proportion of emigrants, many skilled and semiskilled urban tradesmen were inspired to emigrate for periods of a year or less to take advantage of high wages at certain times in growing

American towns. Indeed, it is estimated that by the end of the nineteenth century around one-third of emigrants returned to Scotland. The Highlands were affected by the Clearances in the same way as Ireland during the potato famine of the 1840s. Many Scots died, and more emigrated. After the turn of the twentieth century, Scotland's iron and coal industries were almost exhausted. The expense of mining made the product uncompetitive in the world market, resulting in more unemployment, poverty, and emigration.

The most important factor in the advent of mass emigration was the development of the steam engine. Steamships could cross the Atlantic in a week, compared to a sailing ship crossing of six weeks. Rapidly expanding railway networks in Scotland and North America allowed people to travel rapidly both to ports of departure and away from ports of arrival. Emigration was facilitated by special "passenger line" steamship companies, newspaper advertising, the improvement in communications brought about by the creation of postal services and the telegraph, and encouragement from the British government via emigration societies.

32

Scotties and Other Dogs

General Dwight D. Eisenhower took his Scottish terrier everywhere with him during World War II. At one point, he told his wife, Mamie, that his dog was the only companion he could really talk to and the only one who would not turn the conversation back to the topic of war. And we all know how important President Franklin Delano Roosevelt's dog was to him. Fala, the best loved and most famous of all White House pets, was born in 1940, a gift to the president from his cousin, Margaret Stuckley. The president loved Fala so much that he rarely went anywhere without him. FDR had several Scotties before Fala, including one named Duffy and another named Mr. Duffy. At a famous campaign dinner in 1944, Roosevelt made his famous Fala speech. "These Republican leaders have not been content with attacks on me, or my wife, or on my sons. No, not content with that, they now include my little dog, Fala. Well, of course, I don't resent attacks, and my family doesn't resent at-

tacks, but . . . being a Scot . . . Fala does resent them . . . He has not been the same dog since."

Captain W. W. Mackie has been called the father of the modern Scottish terrier. According to excepts from Mackie's travel diary, in the 1870s he sought out and acquired prime breeding stock of the then little-known "Scotch terrier" from fox hunters and gamekeepers in the Western Highlands of Scotland. He bought a breeding pair and a pair of puppies from a deer forester named McGregor in Argyllshire. From these parents came a champion, "Dundee," the prototype of the modern Scottie.

Scotties have always been popular in America. Theodore Roosevelt had a Scottie named Jessie and his daughter, Alice Roosevelt Longworth, had a Scottie named Sandy. Presdient Dwight D. Eisenhower had two of them. Scotties have been the favored pets of many actors; owners have included John Barrymore, Lionel Barrymore, Humphrey Bogart, Bette Davis, Dorothy Lamour, Bert Lahr, Betty Hutton, Ida Lupino, Walter Pidgeon, Basil Rathbone, and Zsa Zsa Gabor. Ali McGraw, Liza Minelli, and Bonnie Raitt also have Scotties.

Gordon setters are the black-and-tan hunting companions developed in Scotland by the Duke of Gordon. The largest boned and heaviest of the traditional setters, they generally work fairly close to their hunting partners. They are by nature affectionate and loyal, making

them particularly well suited to an active family with children, whom they often adore.

Gordons can move from family room to hunting lodge with ease, as long as they can be with the ones they love; there are an increasing number of dual champions in the breed who demonstrate that it is possible to successfully combine show-ring, field-trial, and even obedience-competition careers. There are an increasing number of "new" competition and noncompetitive activities available for Gordons and their owners: tracking, agility, therapy work, search and rescue, and flyball have all been taken up successfully by modern-day black and tans.

Shetland sheepdogs as they exist today are a relatively young breed. The original stock probably consisted of Scandinavian herding dogs from the same stock as the Norwegian buhund or the Icelandic dog. (The Nordic herding dogs are rarely mentioned in the history of the breed, but there is every reason to assume that the original Norse settlers brought along their dogs as well as their small sheep, cows, and horses. There is archaeological evidence of such dogs dating from before the transfer of the Shetland Islands to Scotland.)

"Collie" is an all-inclusive Scottish term for a sheepdog. Developed in Scotland from local sheepdogs, particularly the old English sheepdog, with a possible influx of genes from the Poland lowland sheepdog and the komondor, the "Beardie" is a sturdy representative of the pas-

toral group. There were probably originally two types of bearded collie. One was smaller and lighter boned and was used for herding flocks in the Highlands and for huntaways. Huntaways involved the dog and the shepherd working behind the sheep and having the dog work back and forth, barking continuously. This drove out the lost or hiding flock members. The other version of the beardie was a heavier boned dog with a solid black coat. This type of beardie was used for droving in the Lowlands. The modern bearded collie is believed to be an amalgamation of these two versions of herding dog. The history of the bearded collie is not clearly defined. There are records of beardie type dogs droving cattle from the north.

It is believed that rough collies are descended from native Scottish dogs and dogs that accompanied the Roman invaders in 50 B.C. They probably take their name from a type of black sheep, colleys, bred in the Lowlands of Scotland. In the 1860s, Queen Victoria became entranced with these dogs when she visited her Scottish estate at Balmoral and took some back with her to Windsor Castle. Known at that time as the Scottish sheepdog, the collie first entered the show-ring at the Birmingham Dog Society Show and was soon highly sought after. By 1878, America followed suit. In the 1940s, the breed shot to even greater fame when a rough collie was chosen to star as Lassie, from the much-loved series of films based on Eric Knight's classic novel *Lassie Come Home.* The film Lassie was really a "Laddie."

West Highland white terriers were bred to hunt otters, foxes, and vermin. They share their ancestry with the Scottie, cairn, and dandie dinmont terriers. From the rough-coated terrier stock in Scotland, white whelps were selected to form this breed. Records show that James I, king of England in the 1620s, requested some "little white earth dogges" out of Argyleshire in Scotland, and these were possibly Westies. Col. Malcolm of Poltalloch, Argyleshire, accidentally shot and killed his favorite terrier (a dark colored one) and vowed from then on only to have white dogs. He may have been the originator of the Highland terrier, but at that time they were called poltalloch terriers. The Duke of Argyll's estate at Dumbartonshire was called Roseneath and in the nineteenth century, Westies were known as roseneath terriers in honor of his patronage and interest. In the first organized dog shows in the late 1800s, they were known as white Scottish terrier cairns. Terriers are natives of the western islands of Scotland and, in particular, the Isle of Skye, and have been known since the 1500s. The breed was named after the rocks (cairns) that were erected to mark a boundary or grave. These rocks became the favorite hiding place for foxes and other pests and a small but fearless terrier was required to rout out the vermin. From a large variety of terrier type dogs, four distinct breeds slowly emerged: the cairn, Skye, West Highland white, and Scottish. Until cairns were accepted by the Kennel Club of Great Britain in 1910, the breed was virtually unheard of outside its home. When first exhibited, cairns were

called "short haired Skye terriers" since Skyes were already established, but the Skye fanciers were outraged; hence the name "cairn" came into being. They reached American shores in 1913.

The deerhound, the "Royal Dog of Scotland," has a long history. The earliest names bestowed on it are so mixed that no one really knows whether the deerhound was at one time identical with the ancient Irish wolfdog and, in the course of centuries, bred to a type better suited to hunt deer, or whether, as some writers claim, he is the descendant of the hounds of the Picts. Very early descriptive names were used to identify the purpose of the dog rather than to identify species. We find such names as "Irish wolf dog," "Scotch greyhound," "rough greyhound," and "Highland deerhound."

Throughout the ages, great value has been set on the deerhound. The history of the breed is filled with romance from the Age of Chivalry, when no one of rank lower than an earl was permitted to possess a deerhound. A noble lord condemned to death might purchase his reprieve with an offering of deerhounds. Records of the Middle Ages allude repeatedly to the delightful attributes of this charming hound, his tremendous courage in the chase, and his gentle dignity in the home.

The hounds were usually used for hunting singly or in pairs, and for centuries served as the companions and guards of Highland chieftains. The grace, dignity, and beauty of the deerhound have been faithfully depicted in many drawings, and Sir Walter Scott, who owned the famous

deerhound "Maida" wrote many enthusiastic tributes to the breed, which he describes as "the most perfect creature of Heaven." So highly has the deerhound been esteemed that the desire for exclusive ownership has at many times endangered the continuance of the breed. As the larger beasts of the chase became extinct or rare in England and southern Scotland, the more delicate, smooth greyhound took the place of the larger deerhound.

33

Shetland Ponies

The Shetland pony is one of the oldest and purest of Britain's native horse breeds. The earliest known illustrations of Shetland ponies are depicted on the carved Bressay and Papil stones, dating from around the ninth century. Each shows a man astride a very small pony. The former was found on Bressay, the island off Shetland Mainland, where Lord Londonderry was to found his famous Londonderry Stud in the late 1800s. Most Shetland ponies of today are descended from Londonderry stock.

Many allusions are made to Shetland ponies in documents through the centuries, but our best knowledge of the breed comes from the records kept by the Shetland Islanders and travelers to the islands in the last few hundred years. It is probable that ponies came to Shetland from Iceland with the Vikings, which explains why Shetlands come in most of the colors found in Icelandic ponies. As with Icelandics, they are never

spotted in color. Shetland ponies are some of the hardiest of equines. The essential features of this pony are small stature and hardiness, extra thick double-winter coat, long dense mane and tail, and the ability to thrive on a very poor quality diet—all of which ensured the survival of the fittest.

Because of the islands' isolation, the purity of the Shetland pony, especially its small stature and hardiness, have been ensured. Over the past two hundred years, they have been exported all over the world with remarkable success, due to their ability to adapt to new and very different environments. A Shetland pony, properly broken, makes an ideal ridden or driven pony. They have been the first mount of some famous riders, and can hold their own in competition with larger native breeds.

Shetland ponies did much of the hard work on the islands, from pulling carts loaded with hay or seaweed to carrying home the peat from the hills for winter fuel. Adults and children rode them, just as they do today. Hair from the mane and tail was valuable and used for a number of purposes, including the manufacture of fishing line. Indeed, it was an offense to cut the mane or tail of another person's pony, punishable by a large fine. When a law was passed in 1842 banning the employment of children in coal mines, the Shetland pony found a new market. Mine owners bought hundreds of the strongest colts, mostly black, to pull coal carts underground, where they gained a reputation for being docile, easy to train, and had unequalled strength for their

size. The smaller ponies, which would be called miniatures today, were employed in the smaller tunnels.

Ponies have been exported from Shetland for centuries. By the late 1800s, great numbers had left the islands for Europe and America. Consignments of up to 129 ponies at a time to America were recorded. They were popular as harness ponies and became the foundation of such miniature breeds as fallabellas. The celebrated American horse tamer, John Rarey, purchased five while on a trip to Shetland in 1860, four of which he took back home with him to join his traveling exhibition and form a stud in Ohio.

34

Sports

Even though Scotland is most famous for golf, it has its share of heroes in other sports. Runner Eric Liddell won the 400-meter gold at the 1924 Paris Olympics. His story was the inspiration for the movie *Chariots of Fire.* He went on to spend the rest of his life as a missionary in China and died in a Japanese prison camp during World War II.

Scotland also lays claim to champions in several unusual sports. Scotland's single most successful Commonwealth Games medalist, Alister Allan, was born in Freuchie (Fife) in 1944. In a shooting career spanning twenty-six years, he took part in six Commonwealth Games (1974–1994), winning three gold, three silver, and four bronze medals. He also competed in five Olympic Games, winning a bronze medal in 1984 and a silver medal in 1988, both in small-bore rifle shooting. Following his record-breaking career, he became an international shooting coach.

Motor racing has had some prime Scottish drivers. Motorcycle racer Robert (Bob) McGregor McIntyre, probably the most daring competitor in the sport, earned the nickname "The Flying Scotsman." Born in Scotstoun (Glasgow) in 1928, McIntyre began serious competition in off-road racing in 1948. Soon he turned to track racing and found immediate success at his first competition at Balado Airfield, Kinross. He is most famously associated with the Isle of Man TT race, where he was the first to record a 100 mph lap. He was killed at Alton Parkin 1962. A classic race is held annually in his honor at East Fortune Airfield (East Lothian).

James (Jim) Clark (1936–1968) was a two-time world champion racing driver and won seven Grand Prix races in a row, twenty-five in all, breaking the previous record of twenty-four. Jackie Stewart, a race-car driver born in Dumbarton in 1939, won the world championship three times. In 1997, together with his son, he launched his own Formula One motor racing team.

Champion jockey Willie Carson was born in Stirling in 1942. He became the first "Jockey to the Queen" in 1977. Jim Watt, who won the WBC World Lightweight title in 1979, was born in Glasgow.

Kenny Dalglish, perhaps Scotland's most successful football player, was born in 1951 in Glasgow. Dalglish joined Jock Stein's Celtic team in 1967, and moved to the English team Liverpool in 1977 for a record transfer fee at the time (£440,000). He won the League and European

Cups on several occasions and eventually became a successful manager. He was the first player to score more than 100 league goals in both Scotland and England. One of Scotland's greatest internationalists, he played in two successive World Cup competitions, was capped 102 times, and scored 30 international goals. He went on to manage Blackburn Rovers, Newcastle United, and finally his old team, Celtic, winning a total of four championships as a manager.

35

Tartans

There is great debate on the origin of the word "tartan." It may have come from the Irish *tarsna,* which means "crosswise," or the Scottish Gaelic *tarsuinn,* which means "across." Or it may have come from the Old French *tartaine,* meaning "cloth." What we know for sure is, long before there were individual Scottish clan tartans, the Celts loved bright colors and patterned cloth. Later, the Scots incorporated this love for color into a unique plaid cloth. Only in recent history have particular patterns been associated with particular districts, army regiments, and, of course, Scottish clan families.

Prior to 1700, there is no historical evidence associating particular patterns with particular people or places, but it is clear that plaid cloth was made and worn throughout the Highlands and had been for hundreds of years. By 1746, tartans were so closely associated with High-

landers and clan loyalty that their wearing was banned after the defeat at Culloden until 1782. Interestingly, this was the time when many of the famous Highland Regiments were being formed, and they were allowed to select and wear a regimental tartan (for example, Black Watch). Some of these regimental tartans later became family tartans. When the wearing of the tartan was again permitted, there developed a keen interest in reestablishing or reinventing family tartans, beginning with the Highlanders and later spreading to all of Scotland. King George IV and Queen Victoria both fell in love with the Highlander image as popularized by Sir Walter Scott, and greatly encouraged the adoption of this cultural symbol. Today, there are around 2,800 tartans listed in the Scottish Heritage World Register—including ones for football clubs and individual towns.

The earliest costumes of the clansmen appear to have been not tartan at all, but made of a plain color, preferably saffron. As variety became popular, each clan used the natural dyes most easily procured in its district, and the easiest pattern to weave was one of simple warp and woof. Eventually, a clansman would come to be identified by the local pattern he wore, and before long that pattern would come to be known as the tartan of his clan. It was also of value to the clansmen in battle, who needed to distinguish readily between friend and foe. After the last great Highland conflict at Culloden, it is said, the dead were identified

by their tartans, the clansmen being buried each with his own tribe in the long sad trenches among the heather. To the Highlander, the garb of his forefathers has always been important.

While it is currently considered fashionable to wear one's family tartan, this habit has little historical basis. To fabricate a link to a family with whom you have no connection is considered a serious faux pas in some circles.

By the early 1800s, Scots realized that the knowledge of tartans was being lost and, simultaneously, there was a romantic movement concerning Scotland's past. This led to efforts to preserve tartan designs. Tartans were reconstructed from portraits, collected on pilgrimages, demanded from clan chiefs, and recovered from weaver's notes. The weaving and tailoring industries were especially boosted by the visit to Edinburgh of George IV in 1822. Sir Walter Scott, the historical novelist to whom clans were very important, said, "Let every man wear his tartan." Queen Victoria gave considerable encouragement to the use of tartans.

The significance of the tartan as national dress, worn under various circumstances, created clan tartans for every "name," even those that previously had none. These were often supplemented by hunting tartans of subdued character and dress tartans that were brighter. Further variety was added by fashion, fancy, or trade tartans to fill any niche, including various colors of a single pattern. Dancing tartans originate from the dress tartans. There were even some mourning tartans developed. As the name implies, these are used in connection with funerals, and are usually a design using a combination of black and white.

It is also important to note that the word "plaid" does not mean in Gaelic what it does is English. While *plaide* in Gaelic means a blanket, in some Middle English quotations, *plaid* is used as a verb, meaning "to pleat." Therefore, a "plaid" refers to a blanket or something that is pleated, not the striped material associated with the Highland Scots. The Gaelic word for plaid as we know it is *breacán,* which can mean speckled, dappled, striped, and spotted as well as "plaid."

The first book on clan tartans did not appear until 1819 and listed 100 key patterns, but since then the number of officially recognized tartans has risen to over 2,000—and is still growing. The wearing of the tartan and linking the patterns (called setts) to particular families has done much to unite Scottish culture worldwide and to reestablish our connections with our ancestors and with our fellow "Scots of the diaspora." It is good to care about the past and to connect with our cultural roots and traditions. And there is no doubt at all that the Highlanders invented these wonderful plaids. Neil Armstrong, the first man to walk on the moon, carried a piece of Armstrong tartan with him on his historic voyage.

April 6 is National Tartan Day in the United States—a perfect opportunity to show off your Scottish heritage. Find your tartan and wear it with pride!

36

Thinkers

Some of the world's greatest educators, economists, philosophers, and historians were Scottish. The most famous was John Knox, father of the Protestant Reformation in Scotland. Economist Adam Smith and philosopher David Hume are also known throughout the world.

Born around 1505 to a middle-class family, John Knox left home to study at the University of St. Andrews, where he received a bachelor of divinity degree. In 1536, he was ordained as a priest. During the sixteenth century, the Reform movement started by Martin Luther with his posting of the "95 Theses" began to spread throughout Europe and England. In 1543, Knox became the tutor to the sons of a Protestant, Lord Hugh Douglas of Logniddry. Knox embraced Protestanism, and began to preach Lutheran beliefs—dangerous in a Catholic country like Scotland. In constant danger, he went to England. There he preached successfully in Newcastle and London, and then in Europe. In 1555, Knox

returned to Scotland and was able to preach freely in Fife, Edinburgh, and Angus. During the reign of the Catholic Mary Queen of Scots, however, he was constantly at odds with her supporters and was driven out of Edinburgh several times.

Anyone who has ever studied economics or politics knows the name of Adam Smith. Born in Kirkaldy in 1723, he was a professor at the University of Glasgow. His book, *Inquiry into the Nature and Causes of the Wealth of Nations,* was the cornerstone of the concept of political economy. His name is synonymous with free-market economics.

The economist and philosopher David Hume was born in Edinburgh in 1711. After attending the university, he was introduced to the work of Isaac Newton and John Locke. An agnostic, Hume was a leading figure of the Scottish Englightenment and introduced the concept of social history.

Born in Logierait in Perthshire in 1723, Adam Ferguson was professor of moral philosophy at Edinburgh. He introduced the method of studying humankind in groups and is father of the subject of sociology. William Robertson-Smith, born in 1845, was a professor at Aberdeen University and a biblical scholar. He was charged with heresy and dismissed from his job after questioning the validity of parts of the Old Testament of the Christian Bible. Ferguson became editor of *Encyclopaedia Britannica* and professor of Arabic at Cambridge. Today, scholars consider historical criticism of the Bible valid, thanks in part to his work.

An early Scottish philosopher and theologian, John Duns Scotus was born in Duns, Berwickshire, in 1265. Educated at Balliol College, Oxford, Scotus was famous for his skepticism, which led to the word "dunses" or "dunces" being used to describe those regarded as not being very clever. In 1991, the Vatican elevated Scotus to the status of "venerable," the first step on the route to sainthood.

Dugald Stewart, son of mathematician Matthew Stewart, was a philosopher who succeeded Mark Ferguson as chair of moral philosophy at Edinburgh University. A follower of the "common sense" philosophy, he systematized the doctrine of the Scottish School, including psychological considerations in logic and physics. He published *Outlines of Moral Philosophy.*

Philosopher James McCosh was born at Carskeoch near Patna (East Ayrshire) in 1822 and educated at the Universities of Glasgow and Edinburgh. McCosh served as a minister in the Church of Scotland at Arbroath and Brechin, but joined the Free Church following the "Disruption of 1843." He became professor of logic at Belfast (1851) and after immigrating to America, president of Princeton University in 1868. He was a supporter of the Scottish School of Philosophy, and the work of Thomas Reid and Dugald Stewart.

John Veitch, philosopher, poet, and historian, was born in Peebles in 1829 and educated at Edinburgh. He was appointed professor of logic and rhetoric at the University of St. Andrews in 1860, and then professor at the University of Glasgow.

Mathematician and political activist Hyman Levy, born in Edinburgh in 1889, was the third of eight children in an Orthodox Jewish family. Levy entered the University of Edinburgh to study mathematics and physics. He graduated from Edinburgh in 1911 and was elected a fellow of the Royal Society of Edinburgh in 1916. Between 1916 and 1920, he worked as a member of the aeronautics research staff of the National Physical Laboratory. Levy left the National Physical Laboratory in 1920 and became an assistant professor of mathematics at the Royal College of Science of the Imperial College of Science and Technology, London. He was promoted to professor of mathematics three years later, then, in 1946, he became head of the mathematics and mechanics department. Levy's main work was in numerical methods, differential equations, and statistics.

Richard Burdon Haldane was born in Edinburgh in 1856 and educated at Edinburgh University. He continued his education in Europe and then studied law in London, passing the bar in 1879. He was involved in politics and also became the Queen's Counselor. He was cofounder of the London School of Economics and a lecturer at the University of St. Andrews. In 1905, Haldane was appointed secretary of war and set out to reform the British military system. He was given the title Viscount Haldane of Cloan and admitted to the House of Lords, where he served for the remainder of his life.

37

Thistle and Other Scottish Plants

Scottish thistle is also called cotton thistle or Scott's thistle. These plants produce a large rosette of spiny, silvery-white foliage the first year of growth. The following year, its thick triangular stems grow up to six feet tall and are topped with lavender thistlelike flowers. They prefer full sun and well-drained soil. The thistle may become a weed if the plants are allowed to self-seed freely.

Every school child in Scotland learns the legend of how the thistle, Scotland's national emblem, saved the country in the Middle Ages, when the Scots and Norsemen were at war. Under cover of darkness, the Norsemen managed to land unobserved on the coast of Scotland. Removing their boots, they crept on bare feet toward the unsuspecting Scottish army. Suddenly, a sharp cry of pain shattered the stillness—a Norse soldier had stepped on a thistle. The Scots, alerted to the surprise attack, sprang into action and drove the invaders from their shores.

Thistle was originally the badge of the house of Stuart. The first heraldic use of the plant appears among the property of James III of Scotland; an inventory made at his death in 1458 mentions a hanging embroidered with "thrissils." It was, undoubtedly, a national badge in 1503, the year in which Dunbar wrote his poem, "The Thrissill and the Rose," on the union of James IV and Princess Margaret of England. The Order of the Thistle, which claims, with the exception of the Garter, to be the most ancient Scottish Order, was instituted in 1540 by James V, and revived by James VII of Scotland (James II of England) who created the order in 1687 to reward Scottish peers who supported the king. After James VII's abdication in 1688, the Order of the Thistle fell into disuse until its revival by Queen Anne in 1703. Despite the rebellions of 1715 and 1745, the Old and Young Pretenders (Prince James and Bonnie Prince Charlie) appointed Knights of the Thistle (and Garter) in their exiles. The early Hanoverian kings also made use of the order to reward Scottish nobles who supported the Hanoverian and Protestant cause.

Interest in the order revived when George IV wore the Thistle during his visit to Scotland in 1822. A statute in 1827 increased the number of knights, and in 1987 a statute enabled women to join the order. In 1962, King Olav V of Norway became the first foreigner to be admitted to the order for over 200 years. The Princess Royal was invested in the order of the Thistle in June 2001. The patron saint of the order is St.

Andrew, who appears on the order's badge. When a new knight is installed, a service of the order is held during the week the queen spends at Holyrood Castle. The thistle appears on many Scottish coins.

The cotton of thistle is occasionally collected from the stem and used to stuff pillows, and the oil obtained from the seeds has been used for burning, both in lamps and for ordinary culinary purposes. Twelve pounds of the seeds are said to produce about three pounds of oil. In ancient times, it was thought that thistle had medicinal benefits, supposedly curing cancers and ulcers. The Roman Pliny wrote that a decoction of thistles applied to a bald head would restore a healthy growth of hair. It was also thought to perform as an astringent. Thistle was also considered good for nervous complaints.

Rowan wood, with its berries ripening in early autumn, is one of the most striking and beautiful features of the Scottish landscape. Rowan berries are edible and are widely used for making a jelly for eating with game. The berries were once pulped, boiled in water, and strained, and used as a gargle. Rowan is seen as a magical plant and for some people there is still a strong taboo attached to cutting one down. In the past, rowan was widely believed to protect milk from being stolen by the *shidhe* (fairy folk), and "magic hoops" of rowan were woven and placed under milk storage jugs to keep the milk safe from harm. The raw material of rowan wood was used to make small ornamental items such as bowls.

Gorse is one of Scotland's most characteristic plants and can be found in bloom almost throughout the year, its bright yellow flowers brightening the landscape. Gorse flowers can be used to make green and yellow dyes. With the addition of chrome as a mordant, the yellow can be further enriched to give it a golden shade. Ground down, gorse tips were sometimes stored by farmers over the winter to be used as a fodder if other sources of animal feed became scarce. In Fife, it was considered unlucky to give gorse flowers to another person.

Meadowsweet contains salicylic acid, the active ingredient found in aspirin, and as such can be chewed in order to relieve headaches. This chemical has a sweet, pleasant smell, and the plant was used as an herb to mask unpleasant smells in the home. Meadowsweet is also used as a preservative and flavoring in heather beer, a drink still manufactured today, and based on a recipe over four thousand years old. (On the island of Rum, an ancient pottery shard was found containing traces of meadowsweet, heathers, and royal fern, believed to be the oldest remnant of an alcoholic drink known in Scotland.) Meadowsweet is used in the production of certain wines as well.

Bracken is now the most common fern in Scotland. Often covering vast areas of the countryside to the exclusion of other species, many consider it a weed. In addition, the spores are now thought to be carcinogenic. Although more common in the past, houses in Scotland are still occasionally thatched with bracken. Bracken makes good bedding

for animals and was used in people's beds years ago. It acts as an insect repellant and also makes good packing material. Bracken was also used for protecting the Scottish potato crop from frost. Bracken ashes make good fertilizer; burning bracken and other ferns to obtain soda and potash from the ashes was a significant industry in Scotland until the nineteenth century. Soda was used in the production of glass, and potash was an essential ingredient in soap making. Rights to collect and burn ferns were issued by the king.

Bogbean, a distinctive three-leaved aquatic plant, has been put to a variety of medicinal uses. The upper, shiny surface of the leaves was formerly used as a poultice, and the underside was used for drawing out pus from wounds. In the Glencoe area, bogbean was traditionally taken in the form of an infusion to strengthen a weak stomach. It has also been used as a "spring tonic." On the Isle of Lewis, bogbean has been used to treat heart problems, blood disorders, and asthma, and on Uist, it was traditionally employed in the treatment of constipation.

In Scotland, wild garlic plants carpet many broadleaved woodlands. Wild garlic can be used in much the same way as our domesticated garlic, and there are a number of commercial companies that pick the leaves for use as flavoring for food. Today, garlic is generally accepted by the medical community as being good for the heart. Historically, in Scotland, it was also thought to be useful combatting kidney stones, and

there are records of it being mixed with foxglove leaves in butter and applied to boils to draw out the pus.

Scots used to call foxglove, a member of the figwort family, "bloody fingers," "deadmen's bells," and "witch's thimble." Foxgloves have been used for medicinal and magic purposes for centuries. Its best known use was for heart complaints and dropsy (swelling due to fluid retention caused by kidney malfunction), but it was also used to treat tuberculosis, epilepsy, delirium, and mental disorders, diphtheria, skin diseases, and boils. Most accounts attribute the discovery of the effectiveness of foxglove in treating dropsy to William Withering, an English doctor who obtained his MD from Edinburgh University in 1766; he is believed to have found out about the herbal remedy from a woman named Mrs. Hutton, who had been using it. He published his findings in 1785 as a monograph called *An Account of the Foxglove and Some of Its Medical Uses: with Practical Remarks on Dropsy and Other Diseases.* This was the first published systematic empirical study of a drug. Foxglove began to be used by physicians for every illness they encountered, resulting in overuse. Today, foxglove is an ingredient of many heart drugs.

38

U.S. Presidents of Scottish Descent

It is estimated that well over half of all United States presidents have had some Scottish ancestry. It began with our first president, George Washington—Virginia planter, American general, victorious commander-in-chief of the Colonial forces. Washington's lineage has been traced back to the Scottish king, Malcolm II. So strong was his anti-British stand that at Valley Forge, he was quoted saying "If all else fails, I will retreat up the valley of Virginia, plant my flag on the Blue Ridge, rally around the Scotch-Irish of that region, and make my last stand for liberty amongst a people who will never submit to British tyranny whilst there is a man left to draw a trigger." Washington chose four men of Scottish descent to be members of his first cabinet: Thomas Jefferson as secretary of state, Alexander Hamilton as secretary of treasury, Henry Knox as secretary of war, and Edmund Randolph as attorney general.

Thomas Jefferson, the third president of the United States and a

founding father, wrote the Declaration of Independence. His Scottish ancestry came from his mother, Jane Randolph, and as a child, Jefferson was strongly influenced by the teachings of his tutor, Mr. Douglass, a Scottish clergyman. This influence appears to have continued into adulthood. The Declaration of Independence of 1776 bore striking similarities to the Arbroath Declaration, written in 1320, with an underlying foundation of Scottish principles.

The architect of the American Constitution, James Madison was born in Port Conway. The son of a Virginia planter of English and Scottish ancestry, he had Scottish tutors in his early years and studied at Princeton under the direction of President Dr. John Witherspoon, a Scotsman. In 1776, as a delegate to the Virginia Constitutional Convention, Madison was involved in drafting the declaration of rights and the Virginia constitution; he was also closely involved in the drafting of the bill to establish religious freedom. James Madison strongly believed in the people's right to choose government—a conviction reflected in the United States Constitution. James Madison was elected fourth president of the United States in 1808, and was reelected in 1812.

Andrew Jackson rose from humble beginnings to become our seventh president. Born in 1767 to poor Scottish-Irish immigrants, he was orphaned by the American Revolution. A self-made man with little formal education, Jackson became a lawyer. During the War of 1812 against Britain, he was a major general of the Tennessee militia and in

1815 defeated a British force at New Orleans. Jackson was elected president in 1828 following the first ever direct appeal to voters. His election gave rise to the expression "Jacksonian democracy." During his tenure, Jackson saw himself as the voice of the common man, a direct representative of the electorate. Unlike previous presidents, he did not defer to congress in policy making but used his power of the veto and party leadership to assume command. He was reelected in 1832, and by the time he left office in 1837, he was even more popular than when he was first elected.

The eleventh president, James Knox Polk, had particularly strong Scottish heritage. Born on the North Carolina frontier in 1795, he was the eldest of ten children. His mother, a religious woman of great intelligence, was a descendant of John Knox. Both parents were descended from Scotch-Irish ancestors who had immigrated to America in the late seventeenth century. Polk stood by the prevalent American belief that the United States had a predestined right to control all the territory between the Atlantic and Pacific Oceans, and during his term in office, the U.S. expanded through California and New Mexico.

William McKinley was the seventh child of William and Nancy Allison McKinley, both of Scotch-Irish descent. Records trace the direct-line descent of President McKinley from MacDuff, Thane of Fife. Throughout his life, he displayed strong family values and a sense of moral duty. Both his daughters died young, and McKinley's wife be-

came ill with depression and epilepsy and needed constant care. Her husband was known for his unwavering devotion to her. A distinguished soldier during the Civil War and a prominent lawyer in the postwar years, McKinley was elected to Congress in 1876, where he made his reputation as a leader of the Republican Party. He retired from Congress in 1890, became governor of Ohio in 1891, and in 1896 was nominated for president by the Republican National Convention. Winning the election, William McKinley became the twenty-fifth president of the United States, serving two terms before being shot by Leon Czolgosz, an anarchist, after a speech in Buffalo, New York in 1901. When he died six days later, the country went into mourning. During his presidency, the U.S. became a true world power.

Woodrow Wilson, the son of a Presbyterian minister, was born in Virginia in 1856. His parents were well-educated people of mainly Scots descent, and his grandfather was a Scottish Presbyterian minster. Wilson had a career as an academic, and when he was forty-six he was named president of Princeton University. Eight years later, he was elected Democratic governor of New Jersey, and became president of the United States two years after that. The influence of his Scottish heritage was reflected in many of his policies, including his election program, the New Freedom, which stressed individualism and liberty for all. As president during World War I, Wilson was committed to ideals of peace, self-determination, and prosperity for all. He was the author of

the famous fourteen Points that aimed to chart the course of the world after the war, but his dream of a League of Nations never came to fruition. He was awarded a Nobel Peace Prize shortly before he left office in 1921.

The longest-serving president in American history was Franklin Delano Roosevelt, who had some Scottish blood. His four terms in office as thirty-second president spanned one of the most challenging periods of history, including the Great Depression of the 1930s, the attack on Pearl Harbor, America's role in World War II, and the negotiations for the cessation of hostilities. Roosevelt died in 1945. Under his presidency, the United States gained full recognition as a superpower.

39

Woolens and Tweeds

Monastery records show that in the twelfth century, monks in the border area of Scotland and England raised sheep that were the progenitors of the modern Scottish blackface breed. The monks used the wool of the dun-faced sheep, as they were often called, for their own clothing and exported large amounts to Europe. Later records show that in 1503, James IV of Scotland established a flock of five thousand Scottish blackface sheep in Ettrick Forest. The breed spread from the border areas during the nineteenth century to the Highlands, the islands, and to Northern Ireland. A small number were exported to America and Argentina.

Today, the blackface sheep is one of the most important in the United Kingdom. In 1989, their wool accounted for nearly 40 percent of the total wool production of Scotland and one-twelfth the wool production of the United Kingdom. Scottish blackface wool is used in the

production of fine carpets that are both hardwearing and springy. Some grades of Scottish blackface wool are used in the manufacture of Scottish and Irish tweeds. Other grades are exported in considerable quantities to Italy, where the wool is greatly prized for filling mattresses. In the United States, fiber artists and hand spinners use blackface fleeces for tapestry and making rugs and saddle blankets.

Galashiels has been one of the main wool-textile producing towns in the Scottish Borders for over 300 years. Its wool industry began in 1770, but it was not until 1820s that Galashiels' product of traditional Border blue-dyed (previously gray-dyed) reached its peak. But the products that made the Borders famous all over the world were their checked designs, which originated from Galashiels. Other famous Border woolen towns were Kelso, Jedburgh, Selkirk, Melrose, Innerleithen, Peebles, and Langholm.

Hawick moved from yarn spinning for English manufacturers to hosiery and carpet production in the eighteenth century. The town was also a leading frame-knitting producer by 1794. Beginning in the early nineteenth century, Hawick also began manufacturing woolen products, including the new tweed check designs.

40

Writers

Scotland truly stands out in literary history. Some of its early writers played an important role in the history of English literature, and some wrote childhood classics that we grew up with and still read to our children.

James Boswell, born in Edinburgh in 1740, is best known as the author of the greatest biography written in English, *The Life of Samuel Johnson, LLD* (1791). It describes his journey with Dr. Samuel Johnson—one of the most important English writers of the eighteenth century and one of the most quoted—to the Scottish Highland and Islands. Although a lawyer by profession, Boswell traveled widely in Europe, writing accounts in his distinctive style as he went. The eldest child of Alexander and Euphemia Boswell, he was heir to a respectable estate in Ayrshire. In 1782, upon the death of his father (who was a member of the Scottish Supreme Court), Boswell became the ninth

laird of Auchinleck in Ayrshire. An outgoing man who loved to keep company with the most famous people of the age and wrote compulsively about his life, Boswell left a treasure trove of manuscripts that today provide thoughtful, firsthand accounts of life and writing in Britain during the second half of the eighteenth century.

Writer, historian, philosopher, and literary critic Thomas Carlyle was born in Ecclefechan (Dumfries and Galloway) in 1795. Carlyle was educated at Annan Academy and the University of Edinburgh. He wrote on a wide range of topics from the French Revolution to Oliver Cromwell. Carlyle married the Haddington-born Jane Welsh near Thornhill in 1826. The couple lived first at Comely Bank in Edinburgh, then at Craigenputtoch, a Dumfriesshire farm inherited by Jane, before moving to Chelsea in London. Their home there became the center of a literary circle that included the poets Tennyson and Robert and Elizabeth Browning, and the authors Dickens, Ruskin, and Thackeray. Carlyle became rector of the University of Edinburgh in 1866.

Sir Walter Scott, the Scottish historical novelist, is best remembered as the author of *Ivanhoe.* His Waverly novels formed a perfect picture of the history of Scotland. Robert Louis Stevenson (1850–1894) was the only son of the famous lighthouse designer who did not become an engineer. His works include *Kidnapped* and *Treasure Island,* both of which take place in Scotland. Stevenson suffered from poor health and died in Samoa.

Even the creator of London's famous detective Sherlock Holmes was a Scot. Sir Arthur Conan Doyle, born in 1859, graduated from Edinburgh University with a degree in medicine and practiced in Edinburgh, aboard ship, and during the Boer War. The author of *The Adventures of Sherlock Holmes* (1892) and *The Hound of the Baskervilles* (1902), he died in 1930. (These writers are so famous in Scottish literature that they have their own sections in the People section of this book.)

An Angus man born in Kirriemuir, J. M. Barrie, as he was usually known, went to Edinburgh University, graduating in 1882. After a career in journalism in Nottingham and London, he finally settled down to write in London in 1885. His first novel was self-published and had limited success. He did very well as a playwright, writing for the American and British markets. One of his most successful plays was a stage production of *The Little Minister,* adapted from a novel of the same name written in 1891. This was the story of a Presbyterian minister and his love for a gypsy girl.

The story of *Peter Pan or The Boy Who Never Grew Up* is Barrie's best-known and best-loved work. In 1896, Barrie met the Llewelyn Davies family and wrote a story for their children based on pirates, fairies, and a little boy who would never grow up. The story was close to home; at five feet one inch, Barrie's height was a constant source of sorrow to him, and he was often mistaken for a child as a young man.

Barrie's mother, Margaret Ogilvy, encouraged him. When he was young she read books with him and recounted stories of her own childhood—how at the age of eight, upon the death of her own mother, she became "mother" to her little brother, scrubbing and mending and baking and sewing, just as Barrie's fictional character Wendy did for Peter and the Lost Boys. *Peter Pan* was a tale set in a land inhabited by pirates, indians, and a crocodile with a clock inside it. The story was made into a hit Broadway musical that has constant revivals, and was the basis for several film versions. Barrie died in 1937, and was buried in Kirriemuir, next to his mother.

Kenneth Grahame, best known for *The Wind in the Willows,* was born in Edinburgh on March 8, 1859. Grahame was the son of an attorney who could trace his ancestry back to Robert I. He was orphaned at an early age and moved to England to live with his grandmother, attending St. Edward's School in Oxford. Though he was bright enough, there was insufficient money for him to attend university, so he went to Westminster to work for an uncle before starting as a clerk in the Bank of England in 1879. His career there was obviously good, as he ended up becoming secretary to the bank in 1898. By this time he was writing, and published a collection of stories, *Pagan Papers,* in 1893. A very popular second collection, *The Golden Age,* followed in 1895. Grahame married in 1899, and began writing tales for his son Alisdair. In 1908, these were published as *The Wind in the Willows,* a children's classic and

his best-known work. Its animal caricatures—Mole, Rat, Badger, and of course the inimitable Toad—have delighted generations of children (and adults who have remained children, it goes without saying!). In 1930, A. A. Milne turned the book into a successful play, *Toad of Toad Hall.*

Beatrix Potter was not Scottish, but was born into a wealthy London family in 1866. Her family often traveled to the Lake District and Scotland, and she said that her stories of Peter Rabbit were all inspired by spending much of her childhood in the Highlands.

Top twentieth-century Scottish writers include Archibald Joseph Cronin (1896–1981). He trained in medicine, graduating from Glasgow in 1919, but gave this up to become an author. He is best known for *Adventures in Two Worlds* (1952), which gave rise to the radio and TV series *Dr Finlay's Casebook.* George Mackay Brown (1921–1996), a poet and novelist born on the Island of Orkney, was a prolific writer. *The Storm* (1954) was his first work. John Buchan (Baron Tweedsmuir) (1875–1940), a member of parliament and governor-general of Canada, is best known as the author of *The Thirty-Nine Steps.*

The internationally famous author Muriel Spark was born in 1918. Her best-known work is *The Prime of Miss Jean Brodie,* a portrait of a highly unconventional teacher at an Edinburgh Girl's School. The book was made into a major Broadway hit.

Scotland's current best-selling author, Rosamunde Pilcher, was

born in Cornwall in 1924, the daughter of a naval officer. Pilcher now lives in Longforgan, near Dundee, with her husband. Pilcher found success in writing following service in the Women's Royal Naval Service during World War II. She began writing romances under the pseudonym Jane Fraser, going on to publish ten novels under that name. She has since published more than twenty novels in her own name. Some of the best known are *Sleeping Tiger* (1967), *The Empty House* (1973), *Under Gemini* (1976), *Voices in Summer* (1984), *The Shell Seekers* (1987), *September* (1990), and *Coming Home* (1995).

PART II

PLACES

41

Aberdeen

Aberdeen is often called "The Flower of Scotland." The capital of the Grampian Region, Aberdeen is Scotland's biggest fishing port. The early history of the city is not documented, but a Celtic chapel was established there in the sixth century. Alexander I had his main residence there in the eleventh century, and a charter of 1179 established Aberdeen as a free market. The Cathedral of St. Machar, built on the site of the old Celtic chapel built by its namesake, was built in the fifteenth and sixteenth centuries and is the oldest granite cathedral in the world. In fact, Aberdeen was close to granite quarries noted for their silver gray stones that glitter in the sunlight, giving Aberdeen another name: the Silver City.

Nearby, the harbor town of Arbroath contains the remains of the abbey where the Declaration of Arbroath that made Robert the Bruce the king of Scotland was signed. The town is also famous for the origi-

nal Arbroath smokies, developed by the local fishermen. Arbroath smokies are small haddocks, cleaned, salted, and then hung in twos by the tails on wood spits over a fire.

It's unclear as to when rolls were first made in Scotland, but wherever they came from they have subsequently become an Aberdeen speciality. If you visit the northeast of Scotland, you will find Aberdeen rolls on sale in every bakery, corner shop, and supermarket. Authentic Aberdeen rolls contain four ounces of pure lard.

42

Ayr

Ayr and Ayrshire County is best known for its most famous resident, Scottish national poet Robert Burns. The house where he was born is in Alloway, just south of Ayr. His father is buried in the entrance to the cemetery. Tam o'Shanter is said to have looked out of the window of the old church at a witches' sabbath and seen the devil. Many other monuments mark the poet's life in Alloway. A monument built in 1823 displays exhibits about Burns.

Ayrshire County is in the center of the Scottish Lowlands, facing the Island of Arran. Ayrshire is also the home of the Johnny Walker distillery, one of Scotland's best-known whiskys. Culzear Castle, south of Ayr is the best place to see the work of one of Scotland's premier architects. Robert Adam was commissioned to rebuild Culzear, originally built as a fortress, in Classical Italian style during the eighteenth cen-

tury. Carleton Castle in Ayrshire is thought to have been the home of the knight Bluebeard. He is said to have pushed the first seven of his eight wives over the cliff. The eighth wife succeeded in throwing *him* off the cliff.

43

Balmoral Castle

The young Princess Victoria was certainly affected by the growing romanticism surrounding Scotland. Surely she must have read Scott, Burns, and other romantic poets and authors. By the time she assumed the throne in 1837, she was clearly enamored by Scotland. Perhaps this is why Prince Albert bought the estate at Balmoral, which she first visited in 1848. Throughout her reign she took extended vacations at her Balmoral estate.

Still very much associated with Queen Victoria, as well as with the present royal family, the castle was designed by William Smith. Prince Albert was a major influence on its baronial design. The stone is Invergelder granite, which was quarried on the estate. The building was made to house one hundred people.

Clothing styles througout Europe were greatly affected by ruling royal families. Scottish boys were wearing kilts in the early 1800s, Vic-

toria's adoption of kilts as the proper garb for the young princes helped popularize the style as appropriate for boys all over Great Britain.

Lochnagar has eleven summits over 3,000 feet and is south of Balmoral and northwest of Loch Muick. The main summits are Cac Carn Beag (3,786 feet) and Cairn an T'Sagairt Mor (3,768 feet).

44

Dumfries

Dumfries, on the river Nith, is the center of the southwestern part of Scotland's Lowlands, and it is part of the Robert Burns Trail. It was here that Burns spent the last four years of his life and wrote his last verses. His house is now a museum and the Globe Inn still has his favorite chair and an inscription he wrote to one of the waitresses on a windowpane. Although its bridge was built in 1208 and its town hall in 1708, Dumfries did not become a "royal burgh" until 1835.

East of Dumfries, the village of Gretna Green had a reputation as a center for matrimony. Since the age of consent for marriage in Scotland was much earlier than in England, couples under twenty-one often ran off to Gretna Green to take up a short required residence before tying the knot. There are many tales of parents chasing teens across the border to try to prevent elopement. This practice was finally declared illegal

in 1940, but many couples still find the town a romantic place to be married.

Also near Dumfries are the ruins of Caerlacverock Castle, a moat-surrounded fortress built by the English to try to mount an attack on Scotland. North of Dumfries is the red sandstone Drumlanrig Castle, the seat of one Scotland's great families, the Douglas clan.

45

Dundee

Scotland's fourth largest city is set along the north bank of the Firth of Tay. Dundee was once the center of jute and weaving mills, but today it is a center of technology for synthetic fibers, biotechnology, engineering, and instrument manufacturing. The iron bridge over the Tay was built from 1872 to 78. Its two-mile length qualified it as the largest bridge in the world at the time. In 1879, the Tay Rail Bridge collapsed disastrously.

Victoria Dock, a quay in Dundee City opening out onto the Firth of Tay, was begun in 1833 by Thomas Telford. Occupying more than ten acres, it is one of the largest enclosed docks in Scotland. Anchored in the dock is the frigate *Unicorn,* the oldest British-built ship afloat and the most perfectly preserved wooden sailing ship in the world. Scotland's only example of a warship from the golden age of sail, the 46-

cannon *Unicorn* was built for the Royal Navy in the Royal Dockyard at Chatham and launched in 1824. After service there and at Woolwich, she came to Dundee in 1873 as drill-ship for the Royal Naval Reserve, remaining in service until 1968. The Royal Research Ship *Discovery,* which carried Robert F. Scott on his Antarctic expedition in 1901, was built in Dundee.

Dundee is the home of bitter orange marmalade, supposedly created in the early eighteenth century.

46

Edinburgh

Your first view of Edinburgh will tell you why this city has been the capital of Scotland for over five hundred years. The castle, set high, dominates the old town and the famous "Royal Mile" links the castle with the Palace of Holyroodhouse. The eighteenth-century Georgian New Town is beautifully designed. If you are lucky enough to visit during the summer Edinburgh Festival (as my family did when we visited in 1964), you will see these beautiful surroundings made truly spectacular when combined with all the cultural best of Scotland—bagpipes, dancing, hundreds of different colored tartans, food, and entertainment. The castle is used as the site of the Military Tattoo, where troops from all over the world parade up and down to drums and pipes. The castle, complete with drawbridge over the old moat, was also where Mary Stuart gave birth to James VI, later to become James I of England.

Castle Rock is where Edinburgh began. The site was inhabited—and probably fortified—in prehistoric times. When Lothian became a part of Scotland, King Malcolm III lived here with his queen, Margaret, who died in 1093 and was later canonized. Her son, King David I, built a tiny and charming chapel to her memory. It remains to this day, the oldest surviving structure on Castle Rock.

Often damaged and frequently changing hands in the long and punishing wars of independence against England, Edinburgh Castle began to assume its present appearance in 1356 when King David II initiated his ambitious defensive works. In the fifteenth century, King James III began using the castle as an ordnance factory. The prominent Scottish Renaissance king, James IV, added the great hall, but the castle was by then less a royal dwelling than a fortress guarding the Scottish capital. As such it was sacked for the last time in 1573, falling to the English after Mary Queen of Scots was brought down. Repaired and strengthened, the castle became an even more formidable fortress, resisting assaults by the early Covenanters in 1640, holding out for James II in 1688–89 and for George II in 1745. The unsuccessful attempt by Bonnie Prince Charlie's forces to capture it was the final assault in the castle's long history. In 1753, construction of the esplanade began, which is the area that now serves as the ceremonial parade ground where the Tattoo takes place. Sixty years later, the esplanade was broadened and walls and railings were added. During the Napoleonic Wars,

Edinburgh Castle was a garrison for soldiers and it also made an effective prison for French captives.

Edinburgh Castle has not been used as a garrison as such since 1914 though it is still continuously guarded, usually by Scottish soldiers. It houses the Honours of Scotland—the crown jewels, almost certainly the oldest royal regalia in Europe. The castle remains the headquarters of the Scottish Division and houses several regimental headquarters. It is home to a number of military museums and contains the Scottish National War Memorial. The castle was the scene for the 1944 National War Memorial Service, when an honor guard formed on the windswept esplanade and marched over the drawbridge up to the square.

The Palace of Holyroodhouse, the official residence of the English Queen in Scotland, is an essential part of any visit to Edinburgh. Looking onto Arthur's Seat from the bottom of the Royal Mile, it was renovated by Charles II but is much older than his reign. Holyrood was founded in the twelfth century; the remains of an abbey from the period still stand there. Paintings from its long and troubled past hang in the Great Gallery, among them portraits of Mary Queen of Scots and her lover Rizzio, who was murdered in one of the many towers.

Arthur's Seat, the ancient and dormant volcano in the east end of the city, dominates Edinburgh's skyline. However, its imposing figure is something of an optical illusion, as it stands only 250 meters tall and can be walked around in an hour through some fairly gentle slopes. The

walk is well worth the effort, as the entire city of Edinburgh in all its glory stretches out from around the base to the sea in the north and the Pentland Hills—part of the same volcanic range—to the south.

Beneath the City Chambers in Edinburgh lies Mary King's Close, a street that was closed off and sealed up following the plague of 1645 and has since been built over. Today, tours of the close are conducted for tourists, and a number of ghostly sightings have been recorded.

The University of Edinburgh obtained its charter from King James VI in 1582. It was so respected a scientific center that Russian Tsar Peter the Great had his doctors trained there. It was at the University of Edinburgh that chloroform was discovered and the first work on antiseptics was supported. Today, Edinburgh is Scotland's largest university with more than twenty thousand students and a host of buildings scattered throughout the southern part of the city. Moray House College of Education (founded in 1835), with its campuses at Holyrood and Barnton, became part of the university in 1998. The Old College, on South Bridge, is a dramatic building by Adam and Playfair. New College houses the Divinity Faculty, which was built in 1846 to allow students belonging to the Free Church of Scotland, which had broken from the established Church in 1843, to be separately educated. Edinburgh University has had a remarkable number of the famous among its staff, graduates, and rectors.

47

Fife

The Fife peninsula runs from the Forth estuary to the Firth of Tay in the north. This was originally a Pict area and trading center during the Middle Ages. The most popular site in Fife is the town of Culross, a preserved settlement with cobbled alleys and whitewashed houses. Culross Abbey was founded in 1217.

Fife has a long history of association with the Scottish monarchy, so much so that its people fiercely defend its right to be known as the "Kingdom of Fife." The region is home to Scotland's ancient capital, Dunfermline, where Robert the Bruce was buried, and is also the "Home of Golf" (St. Andrews). It is said that all the people of Fife are descended from one man, Conall Cerr, a great grandson of Aiden, King of Forth (a contemporary of St. Kentigern). In 838 A.D., MacDuff became the first thane of Fife. Several other clans and families sprang

from this line of Celtic dignitaries; for example, the MacIntoshes and the Weems (Wemys).

In 1896, there were fifty-seven working coal mines in Fife. In 1948, the town of Glenrothes was founded as one of the first "new towns" to provide better quality housing for miners. Although the mining industry did not thrive, the technology-manufacturing sector expanded rapidly.

In 1975, Fife almost disappeared in the local government reorganization ordered by Westminster. The county was to be split half to the north and half to the south, but the Kingdom of Fife fought a vigorous campaign backed by an ancient royal charter. Fife was the only part of the U.K. to win against the Westminster Parliament.

48

Firth of Clyde

Since at least the 1700s, the waterfalls of the Clyde have been regarded as some of the most impressive in Northern Europe. Rocky gorges with overhanging trees, myriad ferns, and mossy vegetation have inspired many of Scotland's poets—Burns, Scott, Gray, Southey, and others. The Wordsworths spent a great deal of time in Scotland, and Dorothy Wordsworth wrote "The majesty and strength of the water, for I had never before seen so large a cataract, struck me with astonishment which died giving way to more delightful feelings."

The Clyde falls became well known to artists as well. The famous landscape painter J.M.W. Turner visited a couple of years before the Wordsworths, and thirty years previously the Scottish painter Jacob More had painted Bonnington, Cora, and Stonebyres Linns, which rank among the best examples of Scottish painting.

Extending southward into the Firth of Clyde, the island of Bute lies

between the Cowal Peninsula and the Isle of Arran. It has an area of 30,188 acres and is largely owned by the Bute Estate. Loch Fada, which cuts diagonally across the center of the island, forms part of the Highland Boundary Fault, separating a wild, hilly landscape of Dalradian Schists to the north from the more reproductive arable land on old red sandstone to the south. Bute has a unique long-tailed field mouse and a trial reintroduction of the European beaver took place here in 1875. Rothesay, the main town on the island, is linked by ferry to Wemyss Bay and Rhubodach, at the northern tip of Bute, and is connected by ferry to Colintraive on the opposite side of the narrow Kyles of Bute. Places of interest include Mount Stuart House and Gardens, Rothesay Castle, Kames Castle, St. Blane's Chapel, St. Mary's Chapel, Bute Museum, and the settlements of Port Bannatyne, Kerrycroy, Kingarth, and Kilchattan Bay.

49

Firth of Forth

Situated at Queensferry and spanning the Firth of Forth some ten miles northwest of Edinburgh, the Forth Rail Bridge is one of Scotland's most recognizable landmarks—the world's first major steel bridge and one of the greatest achievements of nineteenth-century civil engineering. Although ferries had been crossing the Forth estuary for centuries before, the spread of the railways in Victorian times made improved communications across the Firth of Forth imperative. In 1873, the Forth Bridge Railway Company was formed and construction began ten years later. A balanced cantilever principle was adopted, using three enormous diamond-shaped steel towers connected by "suspended" girder spans resting on cantilever ends and secured by man-size pins. Taking seven years to complete—and costing the lives of fifty-seven men in the process—the bridge's construction involved the use of 54,000 tons of steel, 640,000 cubic feet of Aberdeen granite, and around 6.5 million

rivets. The last "golden" rivet was driven home by the Prince of Wales (later Edward VII) in March 1890, after which time the bridge became a vital artery linking London, Edinburgh, Dundee, and Aberdeen, opening up Scotland's northeast to trade and tourism as never before.

50

Fort William and Ben Nevis

The highest mountain in Scotland, Ben Nevis (4,406 feet high) is the main attraction of the area, which also contains Loch Morar, Scotland's deepest lake.

Fort William is the largest town in the West Highlands of Scotland and is the commercial center of Lochaber, an area renowned for magnificent scenery with an important history. Fort William derives its name from the military fort built by William of Orange in the seventeenth century to station English soldiers sent to control the rebellious Jacobite Highlanders. It was demolished to allow for new railway lines at the end of the nineteenth century. The Ben Nevis distillery was founded in 1825 by John MacDonald ("Long John").

Today, Fort William is a bustling town at the foot of Ben Nevis by the shore of Loch Linnhe, a deep sea lake. The town's population is

around twelve thousand and it is a major center for hikers and naturalists. Glen Nevis nearby forms the valley at the eastern side of Ben Nevis. The West Highland Museum displays artifacts, furniture, painting, and tools used in whisky-making during the nineteenth century.

51

Glamis Castle

Glamis is the home of the Earls of Strathmore and Kinghorne, and the childhood home of the late Queen Mother.

In 1606, William Shakespeare wrote and staged his play *Macbeth,* a dramatic tragedy set in Glamis Castle. Macbeth is referred to as Thane of Glamis several times, although research shows that Glamis did not become a thaneage until 1264.

It is possible that Shakespeare himself may have visited Glamis, although there is no record of it.

In 1599, Queen Elizabeth of England sent a theater company to Aberdeen to perform for King James VI of Scotland. According to Holinshed, author of *The Chronicles of England, Scotland and Ireland,* written in 1587, King James was supposed to be a descendant of Banquo, the Scottish general and companion of Macbeth. Holinshed believed that Banquo was the founder of the house of Stuart. It was well

known that James had a fascination for the occult and witches in particular. Shakespeare is likely to have heard the many ghost stories surrounding Glamis and the story of the burning of the sixth Lady Glamis in Edinburgh. Shakespeare may also have learned of the Glamis family's royal connections. The first earl of Kinghorne, owner of Glamis, visited the court of James I in London, where he may have even met Shakespeare.

The Lyon family began to build the present Glamis Castle in about 1400. There are now two wings linked by a central L-shaped tower. The east wing, which lies to the right of the front entrance, dates from about 1400, as does the L-shaped tower. The west, or dining room wing dates from the late seventeenth century. Daniel Defoe, writing in the early eighteenth century, expressed wonder at Glamis's many spires, turrets, towers, and statues, and likened the place to a city. The entrance to Glamis is through the De'il Gates in the park wall, adorned with beasts and satyrs, which once stood in front of the castle and was reconstructed in its present location in 1775. After a short distance, the driveway turns into a grand tree-lined avenue leading to the castle. In the late seventeenth century, there were outer walls and towers enclosing formal parterres. These were swept away between 1772 and 75 with the intention of remodeling the park in the fashion of Lancelot "Capability" Brown, one of England's most famous eighteenth-century landscape designers.

Finally completed in the early nineteenth century, the park looks like that of an English Palladian mansion and contrasts strongly with the rugged, ancient, and mysterious castle that dominates it. All that is left of the original outer defenses and decorations are the huge baroque sundial, which stands over twenty-one feet high, and the statues of James VI and his son, Charles I.

52

Glasgow

Scotland's largest city is often unfavorably compared to Edinburgh. Though it is an industrial center with what are viewed as bleak buildings and dockyards, Glasgow's name comes from the Gaelic *glas ghu*, which means a lovely green place, referring to its many parks. Glasgow sits on the River Clyde, not far from where the river opens into the Firth of Clyde. Scottish comedian Billy Connolly, who bought a castle near Strathdon in Aberdeen says, "The great thing about Glasgow now is that if there is a nuclear attack it'll look exactly the same afterwards."

Originally a small salmon-fishing village at a crossing point on the River Clyde, Glasgow was founded by a Christian missionary, St. Mungo, also known as the Apostle of Cumbria. Born in Culross in Fife, St. Mungo made Glasgow a major religious center. Mungo's original church was destroyed by the wars that swept through the country in the

years after his death. Today's Glasgow Cathedral dates from the twelfth century and was added to in the years that followed.

Glasgow has also been the site of many battles. Bishop's Castle once stood on the site now occupied by Glasgow's Royal Infirmary. Here, in 1300, William Wallace (of *Braveheart* fame) defeated an army of one thousand English knights who had taken possession of the castle under the English Bishop of Durham with an army of only three hundred men. Two centuries later, the castle was again the scene of battle when two opposing forces fought for control of the Crown of Scotland, then in the possession of Mary Queen of Scots.

In 1451, Glasgow became a university city. Glasgow University is the second oldest school of higher education in Scotland. It was originally built in the High Street area of the city, but was moved to its present site in Glasgow's west end in 1870.

Due to its location in the west of the country, Glasgow was well positioned for shipping to the West Indies and America. By the eighteenth century, many merchants had acquired great wealth by importing sugar, rum, and tobacco. The tobacco lords built fabulous mansions in the city. However, life was very different for the city's poor. By the nineteenth century, the influx of people looking for employment spawned the emergence of tenement accommodations. The poorest families were forced to live in "single ends," one-room homes where the entire family,

often including grandparents, would live together. Many families had to share common bathrooms. However, the struggle for survival generated a common bond between the tenement dwellers and a great sense of community spirit, kindness, and sharing dominated everyday life.

The existence of vast deposits of coal and iron ore in the Glasgow area shaped the next two centuries of the city's history. With the coming of the Industrial Revolution, aided by technological advances designed by inventors such as James Watt, heavy industries such as shipbuilding and the building of railway locomotives flourished. Locomotives were exported throughout the world, and "Clyde-Built" became synonymous with quality and reliability. The launch of the three "Queens"—luxury passenger liners—was the pinnacle of Glasgow's shipbuilding achievement. Shipbuilding is not the great industry it once was, but the area around the Clyde River still has important shipbuilding yards.

Glasgow's botanical gardens, housed in one of the largest glass houses in Britain—the Kibble Palace, built in 1873—contains a marvelous collection of tree ferns from Australia and New Zealand and plants from Africa, the Americas, and the Far East.

53

The Hebrides

The Hebrides are islands situated off the west coast of Scotland, dominated by heather, moors, and a wet and windy climate. There are more than five hundred islands, and only about eighty of them are inhabited. They are famous in Scottish history as the islands where the eighteenth-century pretender to the throne, Bonnie Prince Charlie, took refuge and escaped from Scotland with the help of Flora MacDonald, who remains a Scottish heroine.

The bleak, remote, and treeless islands of the Outer Hebrides run in a 130-mile arc, completely exposed to the gales that sweep in from the Atlantic. The horizon is wide, with white beaches, peat moors, and long, low vistas of sky and water. One of Scotland's largest centers of tenant farming, cattle rearing, and fishing, this is the part of Scotland where you will hear the most Gaelic spoken. As a center of Gaelic culture and

Protestantism, it is also one of the world's last refuges of the strictly held Sabbath.

Tiny Barra is just twelve miles around and ideal for exploring on foot. It encapsulates the Outer Hebridean experience, with its beautiful beaches, Neolithic remains, and strong sense of community. Heading north, expansive South Uist is the second-largest island in the group. The western coast is low with an almost continuous sandy beach, while four large sea lakes cut the hilly eastern coast. The low-lying and soggy island of Benbecula is dominated by the British armed forces' missile firing range. North Uist is half-drowned by lakes, with magnificent beaches on its western side. The chambered burial tomb of Bharpa Langas is the Uists' most spectacular Neolithic site.

Harris, the home of handwoven Harris tweed, is one of the most visited of the islands. The combination of mountains, beaches, dunes, and weird rocky coastline and hills make this one of the most beautiful of the Hebrides. Mountains on a narrow land bridge, sandwiched between two lakes, overshadow the port of Tarbert.

Lewis is the last of the Outer Hebrides. The island's northern half is a low and flat moorland, dotted with numerous small lakes and farms that end at the Butt of Lewis, home to a lighthouse and large colonies of nesting seabirds. The southern half of Lewis is beautiful, the site of Carloway Broch, a well-preserved, two thousand-year-old defensive tower,

and the Callanish Standing Stones, boulders arranged in the shape of a Celtic cross that predate the pyramids by one thousand years.

The Inner Hebrides contain the bigger and better known islands, such as Skye, Mull, and Islay. They have some of Scotland's best scenery and most interesting wildlife.

Skye is the largest of the islands, and contains primeval oak forests. For some, Talisker's malt whisky, distilled in Skye, is one of Scotland's best drinks. Portree is the largest town in Skye, and its harbor is believed to be the spot where Bonnie Prince Charlie and Flora Macdonald said good-bye. Dunvegan Castle was one of the last inhabited seats of the Scottish clan MacLeod, which battled with the MacDonalds of Armadale for control of the island.

The Isle of Mull is treeless, but contains some of the best scenery in the Hebrides. Duart Castle, overlooking Duart Bay, was the seat of the MacLean family.

The islands of Islay and Jura are closely connected, and both are filled with Celtic remains. Islay has some of Scotland's top whisky distilleries—Ardbeg, Lagavuline, and Laphroaig. The island of Tiree gets its name from the Gaelic for "kingdom under the waves."

54

Inverness and the Highlands

Inverness, the capitol of the Highlands, and the area around it has been settled for at least seven thousand years and has seen most of the tribes of the Highlands, from the Picts to the Caledonians to the Scots. It was also in this area that King Brude (king of the northern Picts) had his main stronghold, and where St. Columba converted both him and his whole tribe to Christianity. In 1158, King David of Scotland established Inverness as a royal burgh. Robert the Bruce held several courts in the city after the Battle of Bannockburn. Most of the Stuart kings visited here and Mary Queen of Scots had to find lodgings in the city after the keeper of the castle refused her entry (in 1562, she had the governor of Inverness castle hanged for refusing her entry). It was from here that Bonnie Prince Charlie led his beleaguered army to Culloden to face superior forces led by William Duke of Cumberland (the Butcher Cumberland), youngest son of George II.

Inverness is virtually cut in half by the River Ness as it makes its way from the loch to the sea. In 1822, the spectacular Caledonian Canal was completed, linking Inverness to the western coast of Scotland. The castle, which stands on a hill overlooking the city, has stood on this site since the eighteenth century and the building that can be seen today was finished in 1834. The castle now houses the courts, jail, and police station. Many of the old buildings of Inverness display plaques explaining the history of each. It is a city that brings together both the old and the new. The Inverness area is home to sixty-five thousand people and is growing at an unprecedented rate. As the regional center for the Highlands of Scotland, it is the administrative hub of an area the size of Belgium. It is a vibrant city with a host of high-tech and traditional industries.

55

Isle of Arran

Sheltered from the Atlantic by the Mull of Kintyre and separated from mainland Scotland by the Firth of Clyde to the east and the Sound of Bute to the north, the mountainous island of Arran has a circumference of fifty-five miles. Arran means "peaked island" in Gaelic, and the summit of Goatfell is 2,866 feet high. There are ferry links from Ardrossan to Brodick and, during the summer, from Claonaig on the Mull of Kintyre to Lochranza. The island's principal settlements include Brodick, Lamlash, Whiting Bay, Blackwaterfoot, Pirnmill, and Lochranza. Dairy farming and production and whisky are the island's chief industries.

Brodick is the capital of Arran. The name Brodick comes from the Norse, meaning "broad bay." A few miles from the city is the red sandstone castle at the foot of Goatfell Mountain. As the home of the dukes of Hamilton, the castle was occupied by Cromwellian troops after the first duke was executed during the civil war in 1648 and the second died

in battle just three years later. Brodick Castle eventually passed into the hands of Mary, Duchess of Montrose (daughter of the twelfth duke of Hamilton), who revitalized the gardens. Since 1957, it has been owned by the National Trust for Scotland. Arran is also the site of the stone circles on Machrie Moor, Auchagallon stone circle, Kilpatrick Dun, Torr a'Chaisteil Fort, Torrylin Cairn, and Lochranza Castle.

The String Road, built by Thomas Telford in 1817, crosses the island from east to west through mountain glens. Since Arran lies on the great Highland Boundary Fault, it has examples of rock formations from many periods and has always been a mecca for geologists, including the eighteenth-century scientist James Hutton.

56

Isle of Skye

Already mentioned as the largest of the Inner Hebrides, Skye is 643 square miles in area, formed of a series of lobate peninsulas that are divided by sea lakes. The island rises steeply to 3,255 feet at Sgurr Alistair in the Black Cuillins, which represents the exposed heart of tertiary volcanoes associated with the formation of the Atlantic Ocean. The remains of ancient lava flows outcrop in the north and sedimentary rocks from the Jurassic and Cretaceous eras (young for Scotland) appear in the south of the island. Several formations are rich in fossils, which were discovered on Skye and the neighboring island of Raasay in the nineteenth century by noted geologist Hugh Miller.

The picturesque rugged landscape and relative accessibility make Skye one of the most popular of Scotland's islands for tourists. Electronics and information technology also contribute to the economy, together with journalism through the *West Highland Free Press,*

founded by Brian Wilson in 1972 and based in Broadford. The main town is Portree, which provides the island's only secondary school. The noted Gaelic-language college Sabhal Mor Ostaig is located by Kilbeg on the Sleat peninsula.

Skye is at the center of Gaelic culture and a majority of the islanders speak Gaelic as their everyday language. The population of the island declined sharply through the nineteenth century, when it was included in the Highland Clearances.

57

Loch Lomond

Loch Lomond is the largest fresh-water lake in Britain, twenty-four miles long and five miles wide, and at its deepest point about six hundred feet deep. On the loch, there are thirty-eight islands, some inhabited and even one with a hotel. Loch Lomond is one of the world's most famous lakes, the subject of poetry and song. The lake is crossed by the Highland Boundary Fault and exhibits the physical characteristics of both Highland and Lowland Scotland. Some 200 species of birds and over 25 percent of Britain's wild plants have been recorded in the area.

From the twelfth to the fourteenth century, most of the land around Loch Lomond belonged to the Earls of Lennox. This powerful family owned Balloch Castle, which is still visible today. They also owned castles on Inchmurrin and at Boturich. As was customary, the Earls granted lands to favored families—Arrochar and the northwest to the MacFarlanes, Luss and the southwest to the Colquhouns. The Bu-

chanans and Grahams had land on the eastern side, and the MacGregors held sway to the northeast of Loch Lomond.

There was competition among all the clans. The MacFarlanes, on the rough northern land, were given to night raids on their southern neighbors' cattle (hence the moon was referred to as "MacFarlane's lantern.") Their castle at Inveruglas was destroyed by Cromwell, and another built on Eilean I Vow, ("island of the cow"), where ruins can still be seen today. The Colquhouns share a common ancestry with the Clan Lennox; their castle is at Rossdhu, south of Luss; the small island of Eilean Rossdhu contains the remains of an earlier castle. Part of the grounds now make up the Loch Lomond Golf Course. The MacGregors of Argyll and Perthshire, to the north of Loch Lomond, raided Luss in 1603, following a massacre of the Colquhouns in Glen Fruin (the Glen of Sorrow). For this, the MacGregors' chiefs were executed, and the whole clan dispossessed of their land and their name. To harbor a MacGregor was a punishable offense, so they became outlaws. Rob Roy was the most famous MacGregor.

58

Loch Ness

The area around Loch Ness was settled four thousand years ago. At nearby Corrimony is a burial cairn dating from about 2,000 B.C. However, although some evidence has been found of a fort on this promontory dating from the Iron Age, as well as remains from Pictish times, the earliest written records for the existence of a castle date from the thirteenth century. Loch Ness cuts a great divide along what is called Glen Mor (The Great Glen), a sixty-mile fissure scoured by glaciers during the last ice age. The lake itself is over seven hundred feet deep, and the nearby surrounding hills rise to a comparable height. At the northeast end of the lake, where the waters flow along the River Ness through Inverness and into the North Sea, is the flatter and more fertile land of Moray.

In 1228, the people of Moray rose up against the authority of King Alexander II. By 1230, he had put down the revolt and, as conquerors

often do, established his own loyal men in charge of estates in the area. He granted his son-in-law Alan Durward the lordship of Urquhart, and the earliest parts of the medieval castle of Urquhart (pronounced *"urk-hurt")*, which stand on a rocky promontary on the north shore, were probably built at this time.

After Durward's death in 1275, and following a series of humiliating defeats that caused John Balliol to relinquish his rule of Scotland, the castle, now under British control, passed to John Comyn, appointed by Edward I of England. This was also the time that the Stone of Destiny was taken from Scone to London, and also when William Wallace began his campaign against English rule when he killed an English sheriff at Lanark. In 1297, Andrew Moray of Moray led a nighttime attack on the castle that failed, but sometime later Sir Alexander Forbes retook it for Scotland. In 1303, Edward again took the castle, but his garrison under Alexander Comyn of Badenoch was soon annihilated by Robert the Bruce, who was to be crowned king of Scotland in 1306.

At the southwest end of Loch Ness lies the village of Fort Augustus, separated by the locks of the Caledonian Canal, which runs from Fort William in the south to Beauly Firth in the north. The canal was built in the nineteenth century for two reasons: to create work in the Highlands to slow down the Highland Clearances, when tenants were being driven out of their homes and boarding ships for the Americas, New Zealand, and Australia; and to create a safe passage from one coast to the other at

a time when French privateers had attacked many of the ships that sailed around the north of Scotland, stealing cargo to fund Napoleon's war against the English. Thomas Telford was commissioned to build the canal. It was finished in 1822 but found to be lacking, and reopened in 1847 after an upgrade.

The village was originally called Kilcumein, which means "Church of Cumein." The Irish-born general George Wade was made commander of Northern Britain after the Jacobite uprising of 1715 was crushed, and he was instructed to police the Highlands so there could be no more uprisings. It was with this in mind that he began constructing a series of roads linking together the forts he was building. At Fort Augustus there was a small detachment of men. The remains of the barrack block are still in evidence near the Lovat Arms Hotel. At the site on which the Abbey now stands, General Wade constructed a substantial fort, which when completed in 1730 was named Fort Augustus in honor of William Augustus, Duke of Cumberland, the youngest son of George II. The fort, however, did not fare as well as in the Jacobite uprising. The artillery took up position on the hill behind the fort and with the first shot from its canon found the powder room, causing a massive explosion. Within a short span of time, the fort surrendered without another shot being fired.

In 1867, the fort and its grounds were auctioned off for the sum of £5,000 to Lord Lovat. This was ironic, as one of his ancestors, Simon,

was held at the fort for his part in the uprising, transported to London, and executed. In 1876, his son presented the fort to the Benedictine monks to use as a monastery. In 1878, the first boys school was opened, and in 1882, the monastery was upgraded to an abbey and flourished. But due to a fall in attendance the school doors were closed in 1998, due to the land lease running out and the fact that the abbey was losing money, it closed its doors to the public and to the monks. Although the abbey may be the most historic building in Fort Augustus, there are plenty of other things to see and do. At the bottom of the locks there is an impressive bridge that goes over the canal, and when the yachts and other large vessels wish to pass the road traffic is stopped, and the bridge swings out of the way, using massive hydraulic rams. If you follow the canal down past the bridge, you will reach Loch Ness, and a spectacular view gives you just a glimpse of the sheer size of the loch. If you look upriver, you will see the remains of a viaduct. This was part of the Fort William to Fort Augustus railway; it only stayed open for twelve years, as it lost so much money that it had to be abandoned.

59

Orkney Islands

The home of the Orcadians lies off the north coast of Scotland. Only eighteen of the sixty-seven Orkney Islands are inhabited, and most people live on the mainland—half of them in the town of Kirkwall, which has a distinctly Norwegian flavor. Scotland acquired the Orkney Islands from Norway in 1472 as part of a dowry settlement. King Christian I of Norway pledged the islands as security for his daughter Margaret's marriage to James III of Scotland in 1468. When the dowry was not paid, the islands became part of Scotland. This is a big fishing and farming area, but it is the offshore oil industry that really supports this part of Scotland.

Orkney's human history began at some point before the fourth millennium B.C. Around this time small communities of farmers made their way across the Pentland Firth from Caithness and western Scotland to settle in the fertile northern islands.The daily way of life of

these early farmers can be gleaned from the remains of their houses, burial places, and monuments, as well as the less grand, but equally important, materials such as pottery, tools, and refuse.

Places such as the Knap of Howar on Papay and Skara Brae on the western shores of the Orkney mainland give clear insights into the domestic lives of the farming communities. The island of Papay, around twenty miles to the north of Kirkwall, is home to around sixty archaeological sites. Among these are the incredibly well-preserved remains of the earliest known North European dwellings. These structures, two oblong stone-built houses side by side, linked by a passage through the joined walls, date back to approximately 3,700 B.C. and were continuously occupied by a series of Neolithic farmers for approximately nine hundred years.

The ancient buildings were uncovered in the 1920s when severe sea erosion revealed deposits of midden material and evidence of stone walls. This chance discovery led to the excavation of the site, and after more than six feet of sand were removed, the underlying building was revealed.

The Orkney Island residents had a tradition of elaborate group burials within chambered tombs, such as Maes Howe, Cuween, Wideford, and Quanterness. Men, women, and children of all ages were buried within chambered tombs, examples of which can be found dotted across the Orkney countryside. Analysis of the bones found within

these tombs tells us of a population in which few people reached the age of fifty and in which those who survived childhood usually died in their twenties.

In 1593, the iron grip of the Stewart earls was handed from Earl Robert to his second son, twenty-eight-year-old Patrick Stewart. Like his father before him, Patrick's rule over Orkney was tyrannous, earning him the nickname "Black Pattie." Patrick's reputation for extravagance, arrogance, and greed was matched only by his love of finery—exemplified in the magnificent Earl's Palace. It was Earl Patrick who initiated Orkney's first recorded prosecution for witchcraft. In 1594, less than a year after coming to power, he ordered the first witch burning. Balfour was burned at Gallow Hill in Kirkwall. The Orkney Islands are also the location of Scotland's most northern distillery, Highland Park.

60

Perth

Perth, the capital of Scotland until the fifteenth century, was the setting of Sir Walter Scott's novel, *The Fair Maid of Perth.* The first mention of Perth as a burgh came during the reign of David I of Scotland. The Dominican Friary of the Blackfriars was founded in 1231, and in 1242, Bishop David de Bernham consecrated St. John's Kirk, the parish church where John Knox launched his Reform movement.

From 1296 to 1313, Perth was occupied by the English. There were constant battles between the local clan and with England. In 1429, the Charterhouse was founded by Joan of Beaufort, and in 1437, James I of Scotland was murdered while staying at the Blackfriars Monastery. The founding of the Greyfriars Monastery by the Oliphants took place in 1460, and in the 1540s, the English attempted to invade Perth once again. Oliver Crownwell took the city in 1651 and built a citadel.

The Reformation in Scotland began in Perth when a speech by John

Knox at St. John's Kirk, clearly intended to provoke disorder, resulted in a mob destroying the Greyfriars, the Blackfriars, the Charterhouse, and the Whitefriars. They went on to torch nearby Scone Abbey. The monks and servants who had occupied the destroyed monasteries fled to Stirling in fear for their lives. The regent, Mary of Guise, on hearing the news, assembled an army and marched to Perth. After a short stay she left, leaving a French garrison in place, but they were quickly overthrown.

Perth's two large parkland areas—the North Inch and the South Inch—were given to the town in 1377 by King Robert III and have served numerous purposes since. King James IV (1488–1513) practiced his golf on the North Inch (which still has a golf course today), and horse racing was also held there in the past. Witches were burned on the Inch in the Middle Ages. In 1396, the Battle of the Clans took place on the North Inch; only twelve men survived from a total of sixty from the clans of Chattan and Kay. The battle, which took the style of a mediaeval tournament, was watched from the grounds of Blackfriars by King Robert III, who had a grandstand view of the bloody battle, which, it is believed, was won by Clan Chattan. Robert III, who obviously was not up to the task of keeping these feuding clans in order, soon relinquished the throne in favor of Robert Stewart, Duke of Albany, who ruled until his death in 1424. Four years later, James I returned from captivity to take a firmer control of Scotland. James I held court many times in

Perth and, although it was one of the leading burghs in Scotland and important to James, it is perhaps a slight exaggeration to claim it was Scotland's capital. However, one of his first acts as king was to enable his wife, Joan of Beaufort, to found the Charterhouse in Perth in 1429. The Charterhouse was built just beyond the city's southwestern corner at the time, in an area roughly where the King James VI Hospital currently stands. The Charterhouse was the last royal monastic foundation in all of Scotland and was the first to be destroyed in the Reformation, which began in Perth 130 years later. In 1425, James I attempted to have the University of St. Andrews moved to Perth, but despite James's petition to the Pope, the attempt was unsuccessful.

In recent times, the city was home to important textiles and dyeing industries, and even better known for its connections with the whisky trade—many of the best known brands of whisky have their roots in Perthshire.

61

St. Andrews

The ancient city on Scotland's eastern coast has been a place of pilgrimage for centuries. Legend claims that the bones of St. Andrew, Scotland's patron saint, were brought from Patras in Greece by a monk called Regulus in about 390 A.D. Historical evidence suggests the relics arrived in the possession of a bishop fleeing from England almost four hundred years later. No matter which story is true, their presence in the city that took his name brought pilgrims from all parts of the known world. Christian worship at this spot began around 800 A.D., when the Celtic "Culdees" (Companions of God) established a makeshift church at the harbor entrance. This was replaced with the church of St. Mary-on-the-Crag, whose outline outside the cathedral walls can still be seen. In 1071, Queen Margaret escaped from forces of William the Conqueror across the River Forth. In gratitude, she granted free passage by "Queens Ferry" to pilgrims to St. Andrews. Bishop Arnold began construction of

St. Andrews Cathedral in 1159, but it wasn't until 1318 that the cathedral was consecrated in the presence of King Robert the Bruce. It is even alleged that he rode his horse up the aisle.

Scotland's oldest universiy was founded in St. Andrews in 1413 and golf is believed to have been a popular sport at that time. Certainly it was taxing the minds and bodies of the local population by 1457 when King James II banned the game by act of the Scottish Parliament because archery practice, which was necessary to the defense of the realm, was being neglected. By the beginning of the sixteenth century, the population had grown to 14,000, and at times of religious and commercial festivals more than 300 ships would fill the small harbor and crowd St. Andrews Bay. Local golfers shared the links with monarchs, ambassadors, bishops, and university academics. Mary Queen of Scots and James VI were both visitors to the town.

The arrival of the Reformation stripped St. Andrews of its religious significance. The university was in danger of being moved to Perth and the cathedral once attended by Robert the Bruce lay in ruins when the Society of St. Andrews Golfers, later to become the Royal and Ancient Golf Club, was formed in 1754.

62

Shetland Islands

Shetland's location at the crossroads of the North Sea has resulted in many passing invaders, traders, visitors, and settlers influencing its people over the centuries. The greatest abiding influence came from the Vikings, who arrived in the latter half of the ninth century and swamped the resident Picts. Scottish and Doric influences have also left their mark, as have Hanseatic traders, visiting seafarers, and, more recently, the many nationalities of oil workers who arrived in the 1970s and 1980s.

The first inhabitants of Shetland arrived by boat. Archaeological evidence shows that these Neolithic settlers were farmers, working the land and rearing domestic animals. During the Bronze Age, around 2,000 B.C., climatic changes brought more cold and wet weather to the islands, encouraging farmers to move to the coast. Bronze Age people left their mark in the form of mysterious stone circles and communal

cooking sites or "burnt mounds." The early Iron Age (600 B.C.) was a troubled time when defensive brochs were built to house large numbers of people, animals, and stores. These impressive stone towers are circular with double walls. The best-preserved broch, forty feet tall, is on the island of Mousa. Other spectacular and internationally important brochs can be seen at Clickimin and Jarlshof. By the late Iron Age, some were made into family houses. Walls were built within the brochs to create a wheelhouse with alcoves surrounding a central fire hearth. Well-preserved examples of these can be seen at Jarlshof and Clickimin.

The busy fishing port of Scalloway, Shetland's capital in the seventeenth century, is the heart of Central Shetland. Dominated by the ruins of Scalloway Castle, the picturesque setting was once home to wealthy lords and prosperous fish merchants who built their mansions here. Sheltering Scalloway Harbor are the beautiful islands of Burra and Trondra, linked to the Mainland by road bridge. North of Scalloway, in the Tingwall Valley, is Asta Golf Course, which has magnificent views of the Tingwall Loch, the Loch of Asta, Lawting Holm, and Tingwall Kirk. The area is home to many native wildflowers and birds, including Shetland's first resident mute swans.

Joined to the mainland by the narrow isthmus of Mavis Grind, North Mainland is a vast and magical landscape dominated by Shetland's highest summit, Ronas Hill. To the east lies Sullom Voe,

Shetland's largest sea inlet, and to the west is St. Magnus Bay and the Atlantic Ocean, which has battered the land into a scene of breathtaking beauty.

The coastline throughout the north mainland is remarkable, with magnificent cliffs, extraordinary rock formations, beautiful, deserted beaches, and tranquil, sheltered voes. Inland, the hills are peppered with trout-filled lakes.

Shetland is home to 330,000 sheep. A variety of breeds are reared on the islands, including the distinctive Shetland sheep. It is a small breed, very hardy, and produces soft wool in white, gray, brown, and black. For over five hundred years, the fine, soft wool of Shetland sheep has been knitted into warm garments. Shetland is famous for its locally spun fleeces and for its Fair Isle patterned sweaters, hats, and gloves.

Around the coastline, hundreds of species of birds can be seen, and the towering cliffs are a metropolis for over a million seabirds. Puffins number around 350,000, and they share the sea and the sky with gulls, great skuas (known locally as bonxies), fulmars, gannets, storm petrels, shags, guillemots, kittiwakes, razorbills, cormorants, arctic terns, and many others. The largest seabird colonies are on the internationally renowned bird reserves of Hermaness, Noss, and Sumburgh Head.

PART III

PEOPLE

63

Alexander Graham Bell

With the press of a single button, I can be talking to my mother in Connecticut in about fifteen seconds. It's amazing when you consider that only a century ago, Alexander Graham Bell was just beginning to fiddle with the idea of transmitting sounds through electric wire.

The father of the telephone was born in Edinburgh in 1847. His mother was almost entirely deaf, and Bell discovered that by pressing his lips against his mother's forehead, he could make the bones resonate to his voice. Though Bell spent one year at a private school, two years at Edinburgh's Royal High School (from which he graduated at 14), and attended a few lectures at Edinburgh University and University College in London, he was largely family-trained and self-taught. In 1870, the family emigrated to Canada in search of financial success, and Bell began his career as a teacher of the deaf and mute. In 1871, Bell began

giving instruction in visible speech at the Boston School for Deaf Mutes. Attempting to teach deaf children to speak was considered revolutionary; many people at the time thought that deaf people should be institutionalized and taught to sign. Bell was then appointed professor at the University of Boston as a scientist, experimenting with converting sound into voltage fluctuations in an electric current.

Bell's ideas about transmitting speech electrically came into sharper focus during his days in Boston. As he read extensively on physics and devotedly attended lectures on science and technology, Bell worked to create what he called his "harmonic telegraph." Ever since Samuel F. B. Morse completed his first telegraph line in 1843, telegraphy had blossomed into a full-fledged industry. This new industry meant nearly instantaneous communication between faraway points. While certainly a technological leap forward, successful telegraphy was nevertheless dependent upon hand delivery of messages between telegraph stations and individuals. Also, only one message at a time could be transmitted. Drawing parallels between multiple message and multiple notes in a musical chord, Bell arrived at his idea of the "harmonic telegraph." From this idea sprang the idea for the telephone.

A chance meeting between Alexander Graham Bell and Thomas Watson at the electrical machine shop of Charles Williams was one of the most fortuitous in technological history. Watson was recognized by

his employer as being especially skilled in devising tools that improved the efficiency of various instruments, and was assigned to work with many young inventors. Alexander Graham Bell was just such an inventor. As the two collaborated on ways to refine Bell's "harmonic telegraph," Bell shared with Watson his vision of what would become the telephone. Watson was intrigued, and a partnership was forged. On April 6, 1875, Bell was granted the patent for the multiple telegraph, which sent two signals at the same time. In September 1875, he began to write the specifications for the telephone. On March 7, 1876, the U.S. Patent Office granted him patent number 174,465, covering "the method of, and apparatus for, transmitting vocal or other sounds telegraphically by causing electrical undulations, similar in form to the vibrations of the air accompanying the said vocal or other sounds."

Meanwhile, Bell had discovered that a wire vibrated by the voice while partially immersed in a conducting liquid, like mercury, could be made to vary its resistance and produce an undulating current. In other words, human speech could be transmitted over a wire. On March 10, 1876, as he and Mr. Watson set out to test this finding, Bell knocked over some battery acid that they were using as a transmitting liquid. Reacting to the spilled acid, Mr. Bell allegedly shouted, "Mr. Watson, come here. I want you!" Exactly what Bell shouted—or whether the spilling of acid ever occurred—is a matter of some dispute. Its result,

however, is not. Watson, working in the next room, heard Bell's voice through the wire.

Alexander Graham Bell introduced the telephone to the world at the Centennial Exhibition in Philadelphia in 1876. Brazilian Emperor Dom Pedro exclaimed, "My God, it talks," as Bell read Hamlet's soliloquy over the line from the main building a hundred yards away. The success of Bell's telephone was now the talk of the international scientific community.

In 1878, Rutherford B. Hayes was the first U.S. president to have a telephone installed in the White House. His first call was to Alexander Graham Bell, of course, who was waiting for the call some thirteen miles away. The president's first words were said to have been, "Please speak more slowly."

After inventing the telephone, Bell continued his experiments in communication, which culminated in the invention of the photophone, which transmitted sound on a beam of light—a precursor of today's optical fiber systems. He also worked in medical research and invented techniques for teaching speech to the deaf. In 1888, he founded the National Geographic Society.

By 1891, Bell was testing helicopter models. He quickly moved on to kites as the most stable structure for human flight. Throughout the 1890s, residents of Baddeck were accustomed to looking up at Beinn

Bhreagh, to see the red kites flying in the sun. In all, Bell was granted eighteen patents in his name alone and twelve more with several collaborators. These included fourteen for the telephone and telegraph, four for the photophone, one for the phonograph, five for aerial vehicles, four for hydroairplanes, and two for a selenium cell.

64

Robert the Bruce

Robert the Bruce, born in 1274, was the grandson of the Robert Bruce who tried to get the throne after the death of Alexander III. He was descended from the great King David I, since he was the great-grandson of Isabel, the daughter of the Earl of Huntingdon, who in turn was the grandson of David I. Robert the Bruce was the son of Robert Bruce, Earl of Carrick and Annandale, and Marjorie, Countess of Carrick. After John Balliol's disgraceful submission and loss of his crown in 1296, the earl asked Edward to make him king, as he was next in succession. But Edward turned to him sharply and said, "Do you think I have nothing to do but to conquer kingdoms for you?" To show that Scotland was no longer to be an independent kingdom, Edward removed the Stone of Destiny, on which the Scottish kings were crowned, and had all the papers and documents that might prove Scotland's independence taken to England. Lastly, he made those who had land in Scotland sign their

names on a list to show that they recognized him as their king. If they refused to sign, their lands were confiscated. This list of names is called "The Ragman's Roll" and still exists. It has about two thousand names, including Robert Bruce.

Edward thought he had subdued Scotland, but he was mistaken, for he had not been back in England long when William Wallace stepped into the arena to fight for Scotland. Wallace supported the Balliol claim to the Scottish throne, whereas Bruce was convinced that his father was the rightful king. Bruce was only a few years younger than Wallace, and he emerged as a real hero after Wallace was executed, fighting the English in his place. He adopted Wallace's guerilla strategy, winning back territory, village by village, town by town, until his final victory at the Battle of Bannockburn in 1314. In *Braveheart*, Angus McFadyen portrayed Robert the Bruce as a confused young man, over-influenced by his scheming father. Contrary to what is shown in the film, however, Bruce prepared well for this battle and deliberately drew the English Army to him.

The Scottish Army was made up of no more than six thousand men. They were mostly lightly armed and could call on only five hundred light horses and a small company of Ettrick archers for support. By comparison, Bruce's adversary, Edward II, had amassed the largest army that any English monarch had ever commanded. Some reports claim that it was made up of almost twenty-four thousand men. It was comprised of two thousand five hundred heavy cavalry. Each rider was clad in chain mail and was armed with battle-axes and swords. Each of them also carried a twelve-foot long lance.

Also on the English side of the battlefield were three thousand Welsh archers. This much-feared group of men were experts in the use of the longbow and could fire their arrows with such speed that each archer could have as many as five arrows in the air at a time. The main body of Edward's army consisted of fifteen thousand foot soldiers protected by steel helmets and heavily quilted coats. They each carried a spear, shield, and sword.

Bruce spent a year training and inspiring his men. His greater leadership qualities, married to the patriotic fervor and the fighting nature of his warriors, carried the day. Scotland was free at last.

In 1320, the Scottish nobility signed the Declaration of Arbroath. Its most famous passage reads: "For so long as one hundred of us remain alive, we shall never in any wise submit to the domination of the English, for it is not for glory we fight, for riches or for honours, but for freedom alone, which no good man loses but with his life."

Scotland's Treaty of Independence was signed in 1328 and never again would its very existence be denied. This was Robert the Bruce's proudest moment and a major turning point in Scotland's long and bloody history.

Bruce first married Isabella of Mar and then Elizabeth de Burgh;

their son was King David II. Bruce's reign ended in disgrace when he submitted himself as a vassal to a representative of Edward I of England. Dressed in only a shirt and underpants, he handed over a white wand signifying the surrender of the kingdom of Scotland to the English king. After three years in an English prison, he was allowed to travel to France. In his baggage was found the royal crown and seal of Scotland, as well as money and gold cups.

Just before he died (the possible cause was leprosy) in 1329, Bruce asked that his heart be taken out of his body, and that Sir James Douglas carry it with him to fight against the Saracens in Spain. Bruce's body was buried at Dunfermline. His heart was removed, placed in a silver casket, and taken on the Crusades by the Black Douglas (Sir James), who, just before he was killed in Moorish Spain, hurled it at the enemy. The casket was found under Douglas's body on the battlefield. The heart was recovered and taken back to Melrose Abbey, where the new king, David II (Bruce's son), had asked for it to be buried.

A statue of King Robert the Bruce was unveiled at Bannockburn field in 1964 by Queen Elizabeth to mark the 650th anniversary of the battle. The queen herself is more than half Scottish, because her mother, the Queen Mother, was 100 percent Scottish, and her father, King George VI, was descended from the Stuart kings.

65

Robert Burns

He was one of Scotland's greatest sons and possibly the greatest poet who ever lived. Burns's passion for writing about Scotland, its language, and customs gained him the title of Scotland's National Poet. His fine poetry made him one of the world's most enduring poets. There is hardly a Scot alive who cannot recite at least some of the great man's words, and every year thousands of Burns suppers are held all around the world to honor his memory and keep his name alive.

Robert Burns was born on January 25, 1759 in a two-room thatched cottage at Alloway, near Ayr, where his father, William Burnes, a tenant farmer, ran a small market garden. The family had a life of hardship and poverty, but Robert's father tutored him and sent him to school to receive an education. He also read voraciously and by the time he had grown up, he knew the major works of English literature and also had a good knowledge of other subjects such as French. In 1766,

the family moved and Robert was sent off to Irvine to learn the art of flax dressing. He returned penniless after his flax venture failed when his stock was destroyed by fire. Burns began to think about earning a living by writing. By the time he was in his mid twenties, Burns had become an accomplished songwriter and poet and was showing a particular talent in writing in his native Scots.

Burns's father died in 1784 and he moved, along with his brother Gilbert, to a new farm, Mossgiel, near Mauchline. Burns spent only two years at Mossgiel, but it was one of the most settled periods of his life and he began to write prodigiously. He also met a local girl, Jean Armour, who was the daughter of a stonemason. After a turbulent courtship, they eventually married in 1788. By now, however, Robert was thinking about forging a new life altogether. He considered leaving the farm and starting a new life for himself in Jamaica—so seriously, in fact, that he may have actually bought a ticket for the sailing. Burns decided to try and get his written works published in the hope that the money raised could help pay for the voyage. He traveled to Kilmarnock and invited friends to subscribe to his publication to help offset the cost of printing. When his work *Poems Chiefly in the Scottish Dialect* was published in 1786, it caused a sensation. All 612 of the original copies sold out within weeks. The work contained only 34 poems, but it established his reputation as a writer of national merit. Instead of seeking to make a living abroad, Burns decided to head for Edinburgh, which ri-

valed London at the time in terms of its reputation as a literary center.

Burns did not find life easy in the capital. Members of Edinburgh's then glittering high society found him rough and uneducated, and his social awkwardness and blunt manners often created friction. However, his stay was a success. He managed to get a second edition of 3,000 copies of his book published, earning enough money to tour the Borders and the Highlands. His travels helped him to learn different regional song traditions and cemented his reputation as a songwriter as well as a poet. However, he could not live on the proceeds of his poems forever and, in 1788, he moved back to the west coast. He decided to return to tenant farming and take a 170 acre farm at Ellisland, near Dumfries.

It was during this period, in 1790, that he wrote his most famous poem, "Tam O'Shanter." His writing was as brilliant as ever, but the farming venture turned out to be a disappointment because the land was unproductive. Instead, he decided to try his hand as an exciseman. Burns turned out to be good at the job and, in 1791, finally gave up the farm at Ellisland and moved into the town of Dumfries to concentrate on his excise work. Three years later, he was given the job as acting supervisor in Dumfries. Ironically, despite his reputation as an excellent government servant, Burns was attracted by the ideals of the French Revolution, which was in full swing at the time. His radicalism caused some of his admirers to turn away from his work and mock him, but he soon started to cool his enthusiasm and, in 1794, he joined the Dumfriesshire Volunteers. Writing, working, socializing, and looking after a family were by this time taking a heavy toll. Burns had never really enjoyed particularly good health and started to go downhill. In July 1796, he went to the Solway coast to try and improve his health by sea bathing, but to no avail. He was aware that he was not a well man and, on returning to Dumfries, he died only days later.

What made Burns so unique? Without a doubt, it was the brilliance of his language, combined with the human touch he portrayed through his use of the Scots tongue. He was never afraid to put passion and emotion into his songs and poems, and he wrote in a style that the common man could understand. He established himself just before the old agrarian way of life of Scotland, which had lasted more or less unchanged since medieval times, began to recede—both because of English incursion and the arrival of the Industrial Revolution.

It didn't take long for the cult of Burns to begin flowering. Only five years after his death, the first club was set up to honor his memory. His reputation quickly grew and today there is hardly a country in the world where his poems are not known and his literary skills revered. In his poetry, Burns caught and captured the old Scotland for all time. His best poems, the satires and epistles, are those firmly rooted in the Scottish vernacular tradition; his poorest, those in which he strove to imitate the

English Augustans. As a songwriter his lyric gift was unsurpassed. His songwriting kept him constantly occupied until a few days before his death.

Burns has been all but idolized in Scotland. Burns nights, held around January 25th all over the world, are notable perhaps only occasionally for the wisdom of the speeches or the abilities of the performers: but they help to keep interest in Burns, and indeed, the Scots tongue alive.

Of all Burns's works, probably the best known is "Auld Lang Syne," which is sung around the world every New Year's Eve.

66

Andrew Carnegie

One of the captains of industry of nineteenth-century America, Andrew Carnegie helped build the formidable American steel industry, and in the process transformed himself from a poor young man into one of the richest entrepreneurs of his age.

Carnegie was born in Dunfermline, the medieval capital of Scotland, in 1835. The town was a center of the linen industry, and Andrew's father was a weaver, a profession in which the young Carnegie was expected to follow. When steam-powered looms came to Dunfermline in 1847, hundreds of hand-loom weavers became expendable. Andrew's mother went to work to support the family, opening a small grocery shop and mending shoes.

"I began to learn what poverty meant," Andrew would later write. "It was burnt into my heart then that my father had to beg for work. And then and there came the resolve that I would cure that when I got

to be a man." An ambition for riches would mark Carnegie's path in life, but so would a belief in political egalitarianism that he inherited from his father and grandfather, both Scottish radicals who fought for the rights of common workers. Later in life, after selling his businesses, Carnegie gave away his fortune to cultural and educational causes.

Fearing for the survival of her family, Andrew's mother pushed the family to leave the poverty of Scotland for the promise of America. She borrowed £20 she needed to pay the fare for the Atlantic passage and in 1848 the Carnegies arrived in Pittsburgh, the iron-manufacturing center of the country.

William Carnegie secured work in a cotton factory and his son Andrew took work in the same building as a bobbin boy for $1.20 a week. Later, Carnegie worked as a messenger boy in the city's telegraph office. He did each job to the best of his ability and seized every opportunity to take on new responsibilities. For example, he memorized Pittsburgh's street layout as well as the important names and addresses of those to whom he delivered.

Carnegie often was asked to deliver messages to a local theater. He arranged to make these deliveries at night—and stayed on to watch plays by Shakespeare and other great playwrights. In what would be a lifelong pursuit of knowledge, Carnegie also took advantage of a small library that a local benefactor made available to working boys. One of the men Carnegie met at the telegraph office was Thomas A. Scott, who

was then just beginning his impressive career at Pennsylvania Railroad. Scott was taken by the young worker; he referred to him as "my boy Andy" and hired him as his private secretary and personal telegrapher at $35 a month.

"I couldn't imagine," Carnegie said many years later, "what I could ever do with so much money." Ever eager to take on new responsibilities, Carnegie worked his way up the ladder in Pennsylvania Railroad and succeeded Scott as superintendent of the Pittsburgh Division. At the outbreak of the Civil War, Scott was hired to supervise military transportation for the Union and Carnegie worked as his right-hand man. The Civil War fueled the iron industry, and by the time the war was over, Carnegie saw the potential in the field and resigned from Pennsylvania Railroad. It was one of many bold moves that would typify Carnegie's life in industry and earn him his fortune. He then turned his attention to the Keystone Bridge Company, which worked to replace wooden bridges with stronger iron ones. In three years, he had an annual income of $50,000.

However, Carnegie expressed his uneasiness with the businessman's life. In a letter to himself at age thirty-three, he wrote: "To continue much longer overwhelmed by business cares and with most of my thoughts wholly upon the way to make more money in the shortest time, must degrade me beyond hope of permanent recovery." Nevertheless, he continued to make unparalleled amounts of money for the

next thirty years. In 1872, Carnegie embraced a new steel refining process being used by Englishman Henry Bessemer to convert huge batches of iron into steel, which was much more flexible than brittle iron. Carnegie threw his own money into the process and even borrowed heavily to build a new steel plant near Pittsburgh. He was ruthless in keeping down costs and managed by the motto, "watch costs and the profits take care of themselves."

Although a supporter of labor and unions, in the Homestead Strike of 1892, Carnegie threw his support behind plant manager Henry Frick, who locked out workers and hired Pinkerton thugs to intimidate strikers. Many were killed in the conflict, and it was an episode that would forever hurt Carnegie's reputation.

By 1900, Carnegie's company produced more steel than all of Great Britain. That was also the year that financier J. P. Morgan mounted a major challenge to Carnegie's steel empire. While Carnegie believed he could beat Morgan, the fight did not appeal to the sixty-four-year-old man eager to spend more time with his family. Carnegie wrote the asking price for his steel business on a piece of paper and had one of his managers deliver the offer to Morgan. Morgan accepted without hesitation, buying the company for $480 million. "Congratulations, Mr. Carnegie," Morgan said to Carnegie when they finalized the deal. "You are now the richest man in the world."

Fond of saying that "the man who dies rich dies disgraced," Car-

negie then turned his attention to giving away his fortune. He spent much of his collected fortune on establishing over 2,500 public libraries, as well as supporting institutions of higher learning. In fact, by the time he died in 1919, he had given away $350,695,653. At his death, the last $30,000,000 was also given away to foundations, charities, and pensioners. He was especially committed to the idea that education held the key to success in life. "Man does not live by bread alone. I have known millionaires starving for lack of the nutriment which alone can sustain all that is human in man, and I know workmen, and many so-called poor men, who revel in luxuries beyond the power of those millionaires to reach. It is the mind that makes the body rich. There is no class so pitiably wretched as that which possesses money and nothing else."

67

Bonnie Prince Charlie

One of Scotland's best known heroes, Charles Edward Stuart, the grandson of James II of England, was actually born in Rome in 1720. His childhood in a Catholic family was privileged, but the family's desperation to regain the throne of England and Scotland led to Charles's military training and creation as a pawn.

In 1744, after his father had obtained the support of the French government for a projected invasion of England, Charles Edward, known as the "Young Pretender" and "Bonnie Prince Charlie," went to France to assume command of the French expeditionary forces. Unfavorable weather and the mobilization of a powerful British fleet to oppose the invasion led to cancellation of the plan by the French government. Bonnie Prince Charlie, however, persisted in his determination to drive George II from the British throne and reinstate the Stuart monarchy.

So, in 1745 he traveled to Scotland with a few supporters (possibly fewer than a dozen), and arriving on the Isle of Eriskay he set about rousing the Highland clans to support his cause. Many of the Scottish people believed in the "divine right of Kings"; in other words, the unquestionable right of the Stuarts, chosen by God, to regain the thrones they had lost. The prince raised the Stuart standard at Glenfinnan in Scotland on August 19, 1745, and so initiated what was to be referred to as the "forty-five," effectively the last Jacobite uprising. Among his supporters were 300 from the Macdonald Clan and 700 from the clan Cameron. The rebels quickly took control of Edinburgh and by September 1745 had defeated the king's army, led by John Cope, at Prestonpans. Several victories followed and Bonnie Prince Charlie's army grew in number, at one point reaching over 6,000. Spurred on by the victories, they crossed the border into England and got to within 130 miles of London. Unfortunately, the English Catholics failed to support the Jacobite rebellion, the expected French support never arrived, and many of the English were content with the stable, placid rule of George II. This apathy and lack of support—plus the might of the king's army—forced the Jacobites to withdraw back to Scotland. They had only managed to reach Derby.

The Battle of Culloden, near Inverness, followed on April 16, 1746. The Jacobite army suffered a crushing defeat at the hands of the "Butcher of Cumberland," William Augustus, the Duke of Cumberland.

The battle itself lasted for only about one hour, but a widespread massacre of Scots, many of whom were not even involved in the Jacobite Uprising, followed.

Thousands were killed and the Battle of Culloden went down as one of the bloodiest in Scottish history. The defeat effectively put an end to the last Jacobite Uprising and the Prince was now a fugitive. On the run, he spent the next five months in hiding in the Highlands and Islands of Scotland assisted by his supporters. A ransom of £30,000 (equivalent to $1 million in today's currency) was placed on his head, but despite this no one betrayed him to the authorities. Stuart was hunted as a fugitive for more than five months, but the Highlanders never betrayed him. The greatest manhunt in history culminated when Bonnie Prince Charlie arrived on the Island of Benbecula in the summer of 1746 and met Flora Macdonald. Flora was not an ardent Jacobite supporter but felt that she could not betray the Bonnie Prince. The islanders aware of the Prince's presence on the island were frightened of British government reprisals. Flora helped to spirit him away to the Island of Skye, dressed in disguise as her maid Betty Burke. Legend has it that Flora and Bonnie Prince Charlie fell in love that summer—she did keep a lock of his hair to remember him by—but she may have simply felt sorry for the handsome Prince. He escaped to France in September 1746. Two years later, he was expelled from that country in accordance with one of the provisions of the second Treaty of Aix-la-

Chapelle (1748), which stipulated that all members of the House of Stuart were to be driven from France. For a number of years Charles Edward wandered about Europe. He secretly visited London in 1750 and in 1754, attempting without success on both occasions to win support for his cause. In 1766, on his father's death, Charles Edward returned to Rome under the alias of the "Duke of Albany," where he spent his last years. He died in Rome on January 31, 1788.

Bonnie Prince Charlie's defeat at Culloden had far-reaching implications for the Scots. The English government imposed strict laws, especially targeting the clans. These included making it illegal for Highlanders to carry instruments of war (e.g. swords, targes, and bagpipes) or to wear the tartan and the kilt. Jacobite supporters were either executed or forced to emigrate and their land was turned over to George II, who distributed it among his English supporters.

The Highland Clearances also became law, and landowners now found it more profitable to keep sheep on land that had formerly been used for farming. Many Highlanders now found themselves without a home and there was a surge of people moving from the country to the new, emerging cities. The clan system was changed and Scots scattered all over the world, making intermarriage with other cultures and races inevitable.

Bonnie Prince Charlie's life has been romanticized and he is remembered as a Scottish hero of bygone times, when the clans roamed

the Highlands. His life is portrayed in stories and folk songs recounted and sang across Scotland. A monument erected by Alexander Macdonald at Glenfinnan commemorates the prince and the myth and romanticism that surround him to this day.

68

Sean Connery

Although he had given up his role as British secret agent 007, Sean Connery was still voted "Sexiest Man of the Year" in 1989 by *People Magazine.* And sexy he is, even playing senior roles.

Born Thomas Connery in the Fountainbridge district of Edinburgh on August 25, 1930, he grew up impoverished. The son of a truck-driver, he came from a background very different from that of his screen alter ego. After leaving school, he joined the Royal Navy, but was discharged due to ulcers. He had many jobs, including laborer, lifeguard, and model for art classes, but it was his career as a bodybuilder that led to his representing Scotland in the 1953 Mr. Universe contest, in which he placed third. This in turn led to a job in the chorus with a touring company of *South Pacific.* He appeared in several stage productions, and made his television debut in 1956. He signed a movie contract with MGM in the late 1950s, which led to a string of film roles.

He was cast as the first cinematic James Bond in *Dr. No* in 1962. He won the role over Cary Grant, Rex Harrison, Trevor Howard, Patrick McGoohan, and Roger Moore, even though Ian Fleming was quoted as saying, "He [Connery] is not exactly what I envisioned" as the fictional British agent. However, the film was a success, which led to three more Bond films in the next five years. It was the Bond role that first revealed Connery's gift for exciting women while simultaneously inspiring men. And the secret to Bond? "The person who plays Bond has to be dangerous," he has said. "If there isn't a sense of threat, you can't be cool." Tired of being identified only as 007, Connery quit the role after *You Only Live Twice,* in order to devote more time to his family and to golf. He is an avid golfer (he learned the game for 1964's *Goldfinger)* and in 1996 won the Lexus Challenge golf tournament with pro Hale Irwin.

Connery has played many roles in films over the years, working with such directors as Alfred Hitchcock, John Huston, and Brian De Palma. He won the Academy Award for Best Supporting Actor and the Golden Globe award in 1987, for his role as the Irish cop Malone in *The Untouchables.* He continues to work steadily, despite suffering from various throat ailments. Due in part to this, widespread false rumors of his death circulated in 1993.

In 1990, Connery received the British Academy of Film and Television Arts (BAFTA) Lifetime Achievement Award. In 1995, he received the Cecil B. DeMille Award for "outstanding contribution to the enter-

tainment field," given by the Hollywood Foreign Press Association. In 1997, he was honored with a gala tribute by the Film Society of Lincoln Center in New York and in 1998, received a British Academy Fellowship from BAFTA. He was honored by the Kennedy Center in 1999. He became Sir Sean Connery in July 2000 and received a knighthood from the British government, despite being refused the honor two years previously for political reasons. He has also received awards in France, including the Legion d'Honeur, and the Commandeur des Arts et des Lettres. Connery has been married twice. His first wife was actress Diane Cilento. In an ironic twist, their son, actor Jason Connery, portrayed James Bond creator Ian Fleming in the film *Spymaker.* He has been married to French artist Micheline Roquebrune since 1975.

Sir Sean Connery is among three hundred people to have signed a declaration calling on the Scottish executive to act now to save the Gaelic language and culture before it is too late. The actor, and most of the Gaelic-speaking community, believe that Scotland has reached a defining moment in the history of Gaelic, and that an inadequate response from the executive will ensure the demise of the language.

In the 1960s, he graced the covers of more magazines than the Beatles or Jackie Kennedy. Four decades later, he's as popular as ever with an appeal spanning every culture, generation, and gender. A *New Woman* magazine survey recently rated him the century's sexiest man, above the likes of Paul Newman and Mel Gibson. Although his perfor-

mance as James Bond elevated the superhero to a new standard—a sophisticated, coolly detached killer who makes every move with savoir faire—the man behind that image remains curiously elusive. In 1991, when Connery was awarded the Freedom of the City of Edinburgh from his Scottish hometown (a British equivalent of the key to the city, only loftier), joining such illustrious previous recipients as Charles Dickens, Ulysses S. Grant, Winston Churchill, and Queen Elizabeth II, he was visibly overcome with emotion.

Connery never forgot what it was like being poor, raised in a two-room flat with no hot running water. He knows money means power, and power in Hollywood is everything. He refutes the accusation that he's stingy, saying he's just careful. He used his $1.25 million from *Diamonds Are Forever* to set up a charity trust after he learned of the high unemployment and poverty ravaging his homeland. His next goal is to establish Scotland's first ever film studio near Edinburgh.

As Connery approaches his seventy-third year, he is one of the few actors past retirement age who can still play leading men and credibly escape scorn for May–December screen romances. He has also become subtler, able to say more with a cursory look or a raised eyebrow than most actors can with a long monologue. And he's become more business-savvy, forming his own production company, Fountainbridge Films, named after the slum district in Edinburgh where he was born.

69

Sir Arthur Conan Doyle

Born in 1859 in Edinburgh to Charles and Mary Doyle, Arthur Conan Doyle was sent to Jesuit boarding school in England. In 1876, Conan Doyle attended the University of Edinburgh Medical School where he met Dr. Joseph Bell, the person who inspired the character of Sherlock Holmes. In 1879, he published his first story, "The Mystery of the Sasassa Valley." He served as a ship's surgeon on a Greeland whaler and then in 1881 received bachelor of medicine and master of surgery degrees. After serving as a shipboard medical officer, Conan Doyle moved to Portsmouth to establish a medical practice. He published his first Sherlock Holmes story, "A Study in Scarlet" in 1887. In 1890, "The Sign of Four" was published. The following year, Conan Doyle gave up his medical practice to devote himself to writing. It was fortuitous that *The Strand* magazine was beginning publication at almost the same time, in January 1891, and that Conan Doyle took this opportunity to revive the

Sherlock Holmes of his two successful novels for a series of adventures. "A Scandal in Bohemia" was the first to appear, in July 1891. As Conan Doyle continued to contribute Sherlock Holmes stories to *The Strand,* he became more and more convinced that he should be writing books that would make his a "lasting name in English literature." In November 1891, he wrote to his mother, "I think of slaying Holmes and winding him up for good and all. He takes my mind from better things." *The Adventures of Sherlock Holmes* was published in 1892. During a visit to the Reichenbach Falls in Switzerland in 1893, Doyle chose the location for the "fatal" struggle between Sherlock Holmes and Professor Moriarty. "The Final Problem," the adventure that was to bring the news of Holmes's death to a horrified nation, appeared in *The Strand* in December 1893.

As early as 1881, Conan Doyle showed an interest in Spiritualism. During that year he attended a lecture on that topic, and in 1887 *The Light,* a spiritualistic magazine, published an article by Conan Doyle describing a séance that he had attended. In February of 1889, he attended a lecture on mesmerism given by Professor Milo de Meyer. As part of the lecture, de Meyer tried to mesmerize or hypnotize Conan Doyle, but failed. In 1893, Conan Doyle joined the British Society for Psychical Research. Other members were future Prime Minister Arthur Balfour, philosopher William James, naturalist Alfred Russell Wallace, and scientists Williams Crookes and Oliver Lodge.

Spiritualism focused on communication with spirits. The move-

ment stressed that there was indeed life after death and that communication with those who had "passed over" was entirely possible. The Fox sisters are credited with the birth of Spiritualism. In 1848, Maggie and Katie Fox discovered that they were able to communicate with a spirit that seemed to inhabit their home in Hydesville, New York. The spirit claimed to be a murdered man who was buried in the cellar. By 1855, two million people were followers of the movement. In 1894, the organization was asked to investigate mysterious sounds emanating from the home of Colonel Elmore in Dorset. At night the family could hear chains being dragged across a wooden floor and moaning that sounded like a soul in torment. The family dog refused to enter certain parts of the home and most of Elmore's staff had left.

However, as time went by disorganization within the movement and fraudulent practices lead to the movement's decline. By 1900, Spiritualism had lost its popularity. After the First World War the movement once again became popular as people struggled to deal with the loss of loved ones. In 1916, Arthur Conan Doyle made a declaration that would affect the rest of his life. He stated his belief in Spiritualism. His stunned readers wondered: The man who created the logical Sherlock Holmes believed in ghosts?

In October 1917, Conan Doyle gave his first public lecture on Spiritualism. He wanted to present the facts, as he knew them, for the benefit of mankind. Even though he knew his reputation and career

would suffer, he became an outspoken proponent for the movement. He wrote books and articles, and made countless public appearances to promote his beliefs.

Conan Doyle's already battered reputation hit a new low in the late 1920s. The December issue of *The Strand* magazine featured an article he had written about some extraordinary photos. Two young ladies in the Yorkshire village of Cottingley had taken photographs of things they'd seen surrounding their country home, which they believed were fairies.

Conan Doyle first met Houdini in 1920. Oddly enough, the two men became friends. Conan Doyle wanted to make Houdini a believer in the movement. Houdini must have been flattered by the attention of the famous creator of Sherlock Holmes, and he really did want to believe in the movement. If he could find a genuine medium then he could perhaps contact his beloved deceased mother. In 1922, Conan Doyle and his family were in America for a lecture tour on Spiritualism. They arranged to meet Houdini and his wife, Bess, in Atlantic City. While the couples were visiting, Lady Conan Doyle suggested that they hold a séance. Jean Conan Doyle was an inspired or automatic writer and she felt that she could help Houdini attain his long-sought contact with his mother. The session went well and Lady Conan Doyle produced fifteen pages of writings supposedly from Houdini's mother. While Houdini didn't doubt that the Conan Doyles sincerely wanted to

help him, he did doubt that the message was from his mother. He didn't say anything at the time, but the communication was in English, a language his mother didn't speak. Also, the writings made no mention of the fact that the séance happened on his mother's birthday. Although they tried to put this incident behind them, their friendship never recovered from the rift.

Conan Doyle was a man of many talents. He was a fine sportsman; he played cricket, rugby, and golf, and helped introduce cross-country skiing to Switzerland. He wrote to the newspapers on all manner of topics, was always a strong campaigner for the underdog, and had a keen interest in photography, which enabled him to contribute authoritative articles to *The British Journal of Photography.*

70

Sir Alexander Fleming

It is hard to believe that one of the greatest medical discoveries of all time came about because a relatively unknown microbiologist did not tidy up his laboratory before going on vacation. On his return from his break, he discovered that some mold had formed on the pre-holiday experiment. He saw that the mold, which had developed purely by accident on a culture plate, had created a bacteria-free circle around itself. He was inspired to experiment further and over the course of the next eight months found a mold culture that prevented the growth of bacteria. The microbiologist was Alexander Fleming and he named the active substance penicillin.

Fleming was born at Lochfield near Darvel in Ayrshire on August 6, 1881. In 1906, he qualified with distinction from St. Mary's Medical School, London University. Early in his medical career he became interested in the natural bacterial action of the blood and in antiseptics. It

was while working in this area that the "accident" took place. He wrote a paper, which suggested that penicillin could be used as a topical anti-infectant. This was met with considerable skepticism by his colleagues, and penicillin proved to be difficult to form into a stable and usable substance. He stopped his work on penicillin and concentrated his efforts on matters he considered to be of more medical importance.

At Oxford University in 1939, Professor Howard Flory was conducting experiments with antibacterial substances and their effects on treating wounds caused by bombing. A chemist on his staff, Abraham Chain, managed to isolate pure penicillin, which allowed his fellow researchers to use the substance more freely. Research continued and by the time of the Korean War the use of penicillin internally became widespread and helped reduce the number of fatalities, particularly from gunshot wounds to the stomach. Fleming and Chain were knighted and Flory was made a lord. All three shared the Nobel Prize. As a result of their work, life expectancy grew substantially and their successors went on to develop the science of antibiotics.

71

David Hume

Born in Edinburgh, the son of a Berwickshire laird, Hume was supposed to attend Edinburgh University to study law. Instead, he traveled in England and France, dabbling in philosophy. At the age of twenty-eight he wrote the three-volume *Treatise of Human Nature* (1739). This was too radical a book however, and it failed to ignite much interest in its day. Indeed, it was two hundred years before its true value was appreciated. Hume's main thesis was that morality forms in the early years of life, within the family. Sociability, sympathy, affection, and concern for both self and others are the mainsprings of moral life.

He was a skeptic, but one imbued (luckily) with a highly developed sense of humor. He rejected everyday logic and questioned the idea of cause and effect as a mere imposition of human ideas on the natural universe. Because you see an orderly universe, the theologians of the

day argued, there must be a creator of the universe. Hume argued that we have not seen any other universes to compare with our own.

He influenced Adam Smith, whose account of Hume (an atheist) dying in contented peace offended the religious. He also influenced the philosopher Kant, and predicted the American Revolution. His writings struck a chord with the founders of that great nation. He continues to influence modern thinkers.

72

John Knox

Possibly born in Haddington, East Lothian (little is known of his early life), John Knox became one of the leading figures in the Protestant Reformation in Scotland. After a probable education at St. Andrews, he was ordained as a priest in the Roman church, which by this time in Scotland, as elsewhere in Europe, had become corrupt. Knox worked as a lawyer until 1543, when he became a teacher to the sons of a Protestant lord, Hugh Douglas, and soon became a Protestant himself. This was a time of difficult politics in Scotland. Mary Queen of Scots, a Catholic, had just ascended to the throne, and the many factions in Scotland were divided between alliance with Protestant England and Catholic France. Knox met George Wishart, a Lutheran-influenced reformer, and began to accompany him on his local preaching tours.

Preaching Protestantism was a dangerous job. Patrick Hamilton had been burned at the stake in 1528, at the order of Cardinal David

Beaton, Archbishop of St. Andrews and a very powerful man. The burning of Hamilton was spread over an agonizing six hours, and Beaton repeated this beastly punishment to Wishart in 1546. Wishart sent Knox away just before his arrest, perhaps to protect him, and there is little doubt that this execution had a profound effect on Knox. Three months later, some of Wishart's supporters murdered Cardinal Beaton in his bedchamber. Knox, meanwhile, was moving from place to place with a growing band of supporters. While preaching to the Reformers in the castle of St. Andrews, he was captured by French troops, sent by Regent Mary of Guise. For his heresy he spent the next nineteen months rowing a galley as a prisoner.

After he was released, Knox went to England, where the English Privy Counsel appointed him preacher at Berwick. He was able to strengthen his ties to the Reform movement and concentrate on opposing the Catholic rituals of celebrating Mass and kneeling for prayer. When political turmoil came to a head following the death of Edward VI, Knox fled first to Newcastle, then to France, and later to Geneva. He loved Geneva. There, the Swiss had created a cosy Protestant niche, with abundant law and order. John Calvin was the chief Reformer there, and the two met, furthering Knox's religious transformation.

By now, Scotland had an infant queen, Mary, who lived in France until she was old enough to rule. Her mother, Mary of Guise, ruled in the meantime. By all accounts, Mary of Guise was fairly relaxed, but

some of her prelates continued the harsh dictates of the late and rarely lamented Beaton, thus continuing to fan the winds of religious change in Scotland. Though Knox lived in exile for twelve years, he had been able to visit Scotland twice in 1555 and 1556, preaching in Ayrshire, Edinburgh, and Castle Campbell. In 1558, developing his writing in Geneva, he had a bit of bad timing with a tract named *The First Blast of the Trumpet Against the Monstrous Regiment of Women.* This pamphlet was aimed at the three women who were governing in England, France, and Scotland and were also oppressing Protestantism. Unfortunately for Knox, the Protestant Elizabeth I of England became queen, and she immediately barred him from visiting the country.

Open rebellion broke out on May 11, 1559, when Knox preached at Perth. After a particularly strong sermon, the mob sacked churches and monasteries, and Knox had to leave Edinburgh briefly, where he was preaching at St. Giles as an ordained minister. That same year, Parliament abolished Papal authority. The Mass was forbidden, and Protestantism was established with the approval of a Confession of Faith. Knox continued steadfastly in his thinking and writing, all the more important now that a grave political crisis threatened the throne of England. Henry II of France died and power fell to the Guises. Mary Queen of Scots, was consort to Francis II of France, and support grew in Scotland for the French plan to overthrow Elizabeth I. Knox played this threat as an ace card, and in the spring of 1560 English troops finally

joined the Scottish Protestants. The Queen Regent died in Edinburgh castle, and the French gave up. That summer, the Scottish Parliament met, without royal authority, and the Scots Confession, written in great haste by Knox and others, was adopted. Papal jurisdiction in Scotland was abolished.

The foundations of the new Kirk in Scotland were laid down. The Swiss model, as seen in Geneva by Knox, was used, with church elders, Kirk sessions, and a general assembly. These changes were also the basis of later Presbyterianism. Mary Queen of Scots returned to Scotland in 1561, a young widow. In return for being able to practice her own Mass undisturbed, she allowed for the continuation of reform. This compromise could not sit easily with a man as stern and committed as Knox, and conflict was inevitable. In 1567, Mary was forced to abdicate.

Knox suffered from a stroke and became an old and sick man. In November of 1572, at the age of fifty-nine, hearing of a massacre in France of Protestants, he dragged himself into St. Giles for his last sermon. He died a few weeks later.

73

King James VI

James, the only child of Mary Queen of Scots and her cousin Henry Stewart, Lord Darnley, was born in 1566. When his mother was forced to abdicate her throne in 1567, James became king of Scotland. In spite of the terrible conflicts in Scotland between religious groups and noble factions, James managed to restore order by gaining the cooperation of the Scottish nobility. He struggled to keep Scotland independent of foreign powers, while maintaining the friendship of Queen Elizabeth, whom he was expected to succeed to the British throne. When Queen Elizabeth finally died, James VI of Scotland became King James I of England.

James created even more conflict by knighting his many supporters (especially those whose contributions helped with the royal debt left by Elizabeth) and by accepting favorites. A Scottish Protesant, he was dis-

liked by both Puritans demanding reforms in the Church of England and Catholics. He did, however, manage to keep Britain fairly stable during his reign. In 1611, the King James Version of the Bible was published.

74

David Livingstone

Almost everyone has heard the expression, "Dr. Livingstone, I presume." This is used as a joke when a lost (or inattentive) friend suddenly shows up. The expression came when this famous missionary and explorer was thought lost and then found in the heart of then unknown Africa.

David Livingstone was born at Blantyre, near Glasgow, on March 19, 1813, in an apartment in a tenement building called "Shuttle Row." These buildings housed the workers of the cotton spinning mill located just below on the banks of the River Clyde. When Livingstone was ten he was sent to work at the mill. The bell that called him to work at six A.M. is still attached to the side of Shuttle Row. After work, he attended night school with the other mill children. Some were so tired that they could do little else but sleep, but Livingstone studied hard, often until very late at night.

Livingstone's Christian upbringing prepared him to respond to an appeal by the Chinese Missions. In 1836, He embarked upon a medical degree at Anderson's College in Glasgow. There he studied throughout the winter months, returning to the mill in summer. However, his original plan to become a medical missionary to China was thwarted by the outbreak of the Opium War, which closed China to him. During his studies he attended a meeting addressed by Dr. Robert Moffat, a fellow Scot home on furlough from a mission station at Kuruman, five hundred miles north of Cape Town, South Africa. Livingstone heard of the vast untouched regions of Central Africa and the "smoke of a thousand villages" where the Gospel had never been preached, and soon his thoughts were turning to the great uncharted continent of Africa.

In 1840, under the auspices of the London Missionary Society, Livingstone set sail for Africa on board the sailing ship *George.* On arrival in Africa, Livingstone made his way by ox wagon to Dr. Moffat's mission station at Kuruman. While Moffat confined his work to the region around Kuruman, Livingstone felt compelled to venture north into the unexplored terrain of Central Africa. Isolating himself for several months in a native village many miles from Kuruman, Livingstone sought to hasten his comprehension of the language and customs of the Africans. Availed of this knowledge, he made several early journeys north, primarily to search for sites free of malaria that would be suitable locations for mission stations. Returning periodically to Kuruman,

Livingstone met Dr. Moffat's daughter, Mary, whom he married in 1845. Together they set up a home at Mabotsa north of Kuruman. It was here that a lion mauled his shoulder to such an extent that he never fully regained the use of his left arm.

Livingstone and his family moved farther north to found a new mission station at Chonuane in the country of the Bakwains. Here they met Chief Sechele, who would later be converted to Christianity. Drought forced another move, leading to the establishment of his third dwelling at Kolobeng, just east of the great Kalahari Desert.

From here, Livingstone and his young family made several trips northward. On one occasion, accompanied by his hunter friend W. Cotton Oswell, he discovered Lake Ngami. However, Livingstone's concern for the welfare and education of his family made him send Mary and the children back to Britain. Livingston was increasingly concerned by the slave trade, which despite the 1833 Act of Abolition still persisted on Africa's eastern coast. Africa's great rivers might hold the key to establishing what he called "the highway to the interior," so, with his family safely returned to Britain he set out once more for the African interior. Aided by Chief Sekeletu, his seven-month trek from Linyanti would result in the discovery of the Zambesi River. An emaciated and critically ill Livingstone continued northward and ultimately stopped at the port of Luanda on the Atlantic Coast. Suffering from malaria, which was to plague him for the rest of his life, he was nursed back to health by

kindly Portuguese officials. Realizing that this was no highway to the interior, Livingstone rejected an offer of passage home aboard a British vessel in port at that time. His return journey to Linyanti, following almost the same route, was hampered by torrential rain, malaria, and rheumatic fever. However, after a short rest, again supplied by Chief Sekeletu, Livingstone set out from Linyanti once more, this time following the valley of the Zambesi River. This would lead him to make his most famous discovery. On November 17, 1855, Livingstone gazed in awe at the great waterfall that the Africans called *Mosi-oa-tunya* (the smoke that thunders). We know it today as Victoria Falls.

75

Charles Rennie Mackintosh

Like a number of famous artists, Charles Rennie Mackintosh enjoys more fame now than he ever did when he was alive. In fact, in the later years of his life he lived in fairly strained circumstances, bitterly complaining that the world of art and design was passing him by. Today his designs are priceless and his style is copied by many furniture, jewelry, and fabric designers. The two best places to view his highly individual style are the Hillhouse in Helensburgh, Dunbartonshire, and the Glasgow School of Art.

Charles Rennie Mackintosh was born in Glasgow in 1868. By the time he was twenty-two years old, he had studied art at the Glasgow School of Art, served his time as an architectural assistant, and won a traveling scholarship, which he used to tour and study art in Italy. In spite of all the continental influence, Mackinstosh's design philosophy is

based on Scottish tradition and his adaptation of Scottish Baronial style.

Through a series of exhibitions of furnishings, posters, and graphic designs held in London, Turin, Glasgow, and Vienna, he established the reputation for being at the forefront of modernism and Art Nouveau. Mackintosh never enjoyed great financial success, and he died in debt in London in 1928. His designs, ever increasing in popularity, will be with us forever.

A jewel-encrusted Charles Rennie Mackintosh–designed mahogany writing desk, made for publisher Walker Blackie for his home at Hill House in 1904, was returned to Glasgow after being bought at auction at Christie's in London for the equivalent of $1,573,690. The piece was bought by Glasgow Museums, the National Art Collections Fund, and the National Trust for Scotland and will be displayed at Glasgow's Kelvingrove Museum for eight months of the year and the Hill House in Helensburgh for the remaining four. An ebonized center table also made for Blackie's home but later owned by Andy Warhol brought more than $500,000 at the same auction.

76

Rob Roy

Robert MacGregor Roy was born at Glen Gyle, on the northern end of Loch Katrine in 1671. He was the third son of a clan chieftan who was a lieutenant colonel in the service of King James II. The name Rob Roy comes from the Gaelic *Raibert Ruadh,* or Red Robert, because of his red hair. His great strength gave him abilities with the claymore broadsword that made his name widely known.

Rob Roy dealt in land and cattle and prospered until 1711, when he persuaded James Graham, the Duke of Montrose, to put up a large sum for investment in herding. His chief drover made off with the letters of credit, leaving MacGregor to face a charge of embezzlement. He did not answer to the charge or ensuing arrest warrant and was declared an outlaw. The duke eventually siezed Rob Roy's lands and property and Rob Roy fled with his debts unpaid. With his band of men, at one time almost five hundred strong, he set out on a campaign of cattle rustling,

stealing from Montrose and his cronies. He became a cattle thief who sold his neighbors protection against other rustlers. In the Jacobite Uprising of 1715, Rob Roy, known as the Scottish Robin Hood, mustered the clan Gregor to the cause and led his men in many successful raids around Loch Lomond and Callandar. He was twice captured and made his escape in flamboyant style. All this added to his image and his fame grew.

In 1725, he turned himself in and received a pardon from the king. He died in his home at Inverlochlarig Beg, Balquidder in 1734 and was buried in Balquidder Kirkyard. His memory was perpetuated and romanticized by Sir Walter Scott in the novel *Rob Roy,* (1818), and recently in a major film.

77

Sir Walter Scott

The great Scottish patriot, writer, and poet, Sir Walter Scott, was born in 1771. He was educated at the Old High School in Edinburgh, studied law at the University of Edinburgh, and eventually became a judge of the county of Selkirk and then a judge in Edinburgh.

As a young lawyer, he began to write Anglo-Scottish border ballads and then a number of epic poems, including "The Lady of the Lake" and "The Bridal of Triermain." He then turned to prose and novels, including the twenty-seven *Waverly Novels,* which he wrote anonymously. These historical novels were a huge success and became known in Europe as well as in Scotland.

With earnings from his writing, Scott bought Abbotsford House on the River Tweed, about halfway between Edinburgh and the English border. He then went on to write many historical novels, some of them about Scotland—*Roy Boy, The Heart of Midlothian,* and *The Bride of*

Lamermoor—and others, like *Ivanhoe,* set in England. Scott was knighted in 1820 at the height of his success. He continued writing but a publishing venture left him bankrupt, and he spent his last years writing to pay off his creditors. He died of heart failure in 1832 and was buried in the ruins of Dryburgh Abbey.

Scott can be credited with identifying and nurturing a Scottish cultural identity, as he wrote often about Scotland's history and heroes, usually shadowed by English history. He was also a translator, biographer, and passionate collector of all things Scottish. His home, where he collected items such as Rob Roy's gun and James IV's hunting rifle, holds a treasury of Scottish memorabilia.

78

Adam Smith

Adam Smith was one of the major figures in the eighteenth-century Scottish Enlightenment. No one studying economics can ever forget his name or his most famous work, *An Inquiry into the Nature and Causes of the Wealth of Nations.* A landmark publication, *The Wealth of Nations* was Smith's greatest contribution to the study of economic development.

Smith was born in Kirkcaldy, a fishing and mining town near Edinburgh. His father died before he was born and the earliest records of his life are his baptism papers from June 5, 1723. After attending local schools, Smith entered the University of Glasgow in 1737. Three years later he won a scholarship to study at Oxford, and spent the next six years studying literature and philosophy. A group of friends arranged for him to give a series of lectures in Edinburgh, and these were so successful that he was named to the chair of logic at the University of

Glasgow and then chair of moral philosophy. He eventually wound up as dean of faculty and vice rector.

From 1773 to 1776, he worked as an advisory to Charles Townshen, the chancellor of the exchequer, and spent time back in Kirkcaldy working on his masterpiece. *The Wealth of Nations* presented Smith's views on trade, division of labor, and the pursuit of self-interest in establishing wealth. It became the textbook of those who favored laissez-faire capitalism and its philosophy has had a major influence on trade and industry throughout the world. He is considered the father of free trade economics.

79

Robert Louis Stevenson

Although Robert Louis Stevenson spent much of his life traveling, his Scottish home inspired most of his writing. Fidra, a small island in the Firth of Forth, was the setting of his most famous novel, *Treasure Island,* written in 1883.

Stevenson was born in 1850 in Edinburgh, the only child of Thomas Stevenson, a well-known lighthouse engineer. He studied law, although he never practiced. Plagued by poor health, Stevenson was nevertheless an enthusiastic traveler, and his experiences of different places are woven into much of his writing, including novels, poems, plays, essays, travelogues, and children's literature. One of his most famous novels, *Kidnapped,* was set on Bass Rock. Many of his tales of adventure, as well as his classic *Dr. Jekyll and Mr. Hyde,* have been made into movies.

In 1876, in France, Stevenson met and fell in love with an American

woman, Fanny Osbourne, whom he followed to America, traveling cheaply by immigrant ship and then by train. Unfortunately, the hardships of the journey and the financial debt he endured in Monterey and San Francisco took their toll on Stevenson's already delicate health, and he was diagnosed with tuberculosis.

Stevenson spent several years in pursuit of a healthy climate, traveling frequently between Switzerland, Scotland, England, France, and America until finally, in 1890, he settled in Samoa, where his health improved and he became deeply involved in Samoan life and politics. He died of tuberculosis at the age of 44. His last novel, *Weir of Hermiston,* although incomplete when he died, is widely acknowledged as a potential masterpiece, and one of the finest works of any Scottish writer.

80

Mary Stuart

The life of Mary Queen of Scots was so dramatic that many films and plays have been written about her life. Her reign came during a period of great conflict in English-Scottish history, when the Protestant Reformation was turning Catholic Scotland inside out and many Scots wanted not only to keep a Catholic on the throne but also wanted a greater separation between Scotland and England.

Mary, the daughter of James V of Scotland, was born at Linlithgow in 1542 at the same time that her father was on his deathbed at Falkland. She inherited the throne of Scotland when she was only a week old, and her mother, Mary of Guise, became her regent. Mary was raised at the French court and was married in 1558 to the son of Henry II of France, the Dauphin of St. Germain. Her presence in Scotland was needed, and at the death of her husband in 1560, Mary returned to Scotland to assume the throne. By now, the Reformation had made

Scotland largely Presbyterian by the rule of the Scottish parliament. Mary, a devout Catholic, accepted this, as long as she was given the freedom to observe Catholic ritual and Mass.

As the government sought to find a new husband for its queen, a long and dramatic string of loves, losses, political intrigue, and treachery ensued. Events included the murder of her lover, her Italian adviser Rizzio, who was thought to have been killed by her cousin and husband, Lord Darnley. Lord Darnley was then found murdered, and Mary's lover, the earl of Bothwell, was suspected of killing him. Bothwell was acquitted for the murder and immediately married the queen.

In the end, Mary returned to Edinburgh in disgrace and was imprisoned at the island castle of Lochleven. There she was forced to abdicate her throne. Her infant son, James VI, was crowned king of Scotland.

Mary took refuge with Elizabeth I of England, but the intrigue continued. Elizabeth found her a threat and had her imprisoned. For eighteen years, Mary remained imprisoned while a large Catholic contingent continued to support her, and there were rumors that Mary's supporters planned to kill Queen Elizabeth. The queen of Scots was brought to trial in 1586 for a plan to assassinate the queen of England. In 1587, Elizabeth finally signed a warrant for Mary's execution, which took place a week later.

81

Sir William Wallace

Mel Gibson took a remarkable chance when he decided to direct and star in a film about William Wallace. No other name in Scottish history evokes the deep-rooted feelings of patriotism and defiance of persecution than that of Wallace. *Braveheart* was not entirely accurate, but most of the people who have viewed it have developed a better understanding of that bloody period of Scottish history and what Wallace and his fellow freedom fighter, Robert the Bruce, were all about.

William Wallace turned out to be one of the greatest patriots in the history of Scotland. In his earlier days, however, some of his exploits were not so noteworthy. After a number of escapades, including one in which he murdered the son of the governor of Dundee, he was proclaimed a traitor, outlawed, and was obliged to hide in the surrounding hills and glens.

After the heavy Scottish defeat at the hands of the English at Dunbar

in 1296, many Scots looked to Wallace to take up the cause of Scottish independence. In a series of raids and attacks, he made life extremely difficult for the occupying English noblemen. This included putting the sword to the English sheriff of Lanark, who was reported to have been responsible for the death of Wallace's sweetheart, the heiress of Lamington. Wallace's escapades soon attracted the support of other like-minded Scottish noblemen, including Robert the Bruce, and they combined forces to make life even more difficult for the occupying English forces.

It was only a matter of time before their activities came to the notice of the "Hammer of the Scots," King Edward I of England. He sent a force of 40,000 soldiers and 300 horsemen to bring Wallace and his followers under control. He succeeded in doing this when the two armies came face to face near Irvine in July 1297. Having been deserted by some disillusioned Scottish lords, Wallace was obliged to avoid doing battle and retreated north with his men. It was not long, however, before he got his revenge. At the battle of Stirling Bridge, Wallace's outnumbered and ill-equipped army soundly defeated the English. The battle lasted only one hour. Furious at this defeat, Edward himself took control and in July 1298 brought an army of 12,500 foot soldiers and 2,000 horsemen to Falkirk. In the first major move of the battle, Edward called for his archers and soon the sky was black with iron-tipped arrows. This was quickly followed by a charge of the English horses. The

Scottish defenses were breached and Wallace was obliged to leave the field. His army was duly slaughtered, and the English claimed that they lost more horses than men. Wallace continued to be a hero amongst his own people but was betrayed and taken to London, where he was found guilty of treason and executed.

This did not stop the quest for Scottish independence; fifteen years after the disastrous battle at Falkirk, Robert the Bruce led his army to victory against the English at Bannockburn. This decisive defeat led in turn to Scotland winning her freedom.

PART IV

FOOD

82

Aberdeen Rolls, Buttries and Rowies

The comparison between Aberdeen rolls and French croissants, at least in terms of texture if not appearance, has been made by several writers. It has been suggested that rolls and croissants have a common ancestry that dates back to the end of the seventeenth century in Budapest after the defeat of the Turks. It's unclear as to when rolls were first made in Scotland, but wherever they came from, they have subsequently become an Aberdeen speciality. If you visit the northeast of Scotland, you will find Aberdeen rolls on sale in every bakery, corner shop, and supermarket, and if you taste them you will be hooked forever. The names Aberdeen rolls, buttries, and rowies are interchangeable, so take your pick or even use them all; you'll be understood no matter what you call them. The rolls are roundish, about four inches across and slightly higher in the center than at the edges.

They are anywhere from golden to dark brown in color, and can be either crispy or soft, but must be slightly salty. They also have a very high fat content, which comes largely from butter (hence the name "buttry") with some lard added.

83

Bannock Bread and Black Buns

The word *bannock* originally referred to a round unleavened piece of dough, usually about the size of a meat plate, which was baked on a griddle and used by the oven-less Scots in place of yeast-raised, oven-baked bread. It is now generally applied to any baking item that is large and round.

In the nineteenth century, a sweet bannock made from oatmeal, sugar and cream and cooked in a heavy pan was served to any group of women present at a child's birth. This was called a "cryin' bannock." Later, when the baby first started to cut a tooth, another bannock was made with a teething ring in it and given to the child. Dundee cake—still popular and now often baked in an oven with brandy, currants, raisins, and nuts added—is now a special cake for weddings, christenings, and Christmas. Sweet small bannocks were called crullas (the orig-

inal of the American cruller). They may have come originally to Scotland from Holland.

Black bun is a rich fruitcake, formerly eaten on Twelfth Night. Now it is served at Hogmany. Very much like a Christmas fruitcake, it contains raisins, currants, almonds, and brandy, and is called black from its very dark color.

Inch-thick, unleavened bannocks in the style of the original Beltane bannocks are no longer made; the thickest oatcake is unlikely to be more than ¼-inch thick and they are usually divided up into four *farls* (quarters) rather than left whole. The only large round bannocks made of barley today are Orkney beremeal bannocks, which are soft and aerated with modern rising agents.

Another traditional round bannock with a more recent history is the Selkirk bannock—a yeast-raised, buttery-flavored bun that is made with raisins. The first Selkirk bannocks were made by a baker, Robbie Douglas, who opened a shop in Selkirk's Market Place in 1859 and made a rich yeasted bannock that eventually took on the name of the town. He used the best butter from cows grazing on local pastures and the best Turkish raisins, establishing a quality product with a distinctive flavor. Its reputation was made when Queen Victoria, on a visit to Sir Walter Scott's granddaughter at Abbotsford in 1867, is said to have refused all items on the tea-table spread, save a slice of the Douglas bannock. The Selkirk bannock was to become a favorite of the queen.

Sometimes candied orange peel and almonds are added, and they are particularly popular at breakfast or high tea.

While a number of bakers now make the bannock, the original recipe has been handed down via Alex Dalgetty, one of the bakers who baked for Robbie Douglas. Dalgetty's descendants continue to make the original recipe at their bakery in Galashiels, though Houstons in Hawick now owns the bakery where Robbie Douglas made his first bannocks. Hossacks in Kelso has recently developed a Tweed bannock made with 100 percent wholemeal stoneground flour from Heatherslaw Corn Mill at Cornhill-on-Tweed. Though the original bannock was made with a portion of everyday bread dough, bakers now make up a special bannock dough. Some, but not all, continue to follow the original method of making a "sponge"' dough first, which is left to proof and ferment, developing flavor overnight. Those who follow the faster-rising method produce a less well-flavored bannock. The dough is made with approximately four parts flour to one part butter and lard. It is left to rise overnight and then punched down when the remaining ingredients are added. The dough is shaped into small or large rounds and set to proof again. When they have doubled in size, they are glazed and baked in a hot oven. Baking time depends on the size, from twenty-five to thirty minutes for the smallest to about an hour for the largest. At Dalgetty's, they make between two and three thousand Selkirk Bannocks in a week.

84

Burns Suppers

Haggis, which involves stuffing a sheep's innards into its stomach bag, would be a forgotten dish if it were not for Burns Suppers. Around 1801, five years after Robert Burns's death, the first Burns Club was formed in Greenock, Scotland. In 1805 the town of Paisley had formed a club, and two years later Kilmarnock followed.

The Edinburgh literati, including Sir Walter Scott and Alexander Boswell, son of the biographer James Boswell, held their first Burns Supper in 1815 and resolved to have one every three years. In London, a group of Scots, along with some English poets, had a Burns Supper in 1819. But it was not until 1885 that the Burns Federation was formed, comprised of fifty-one Burns Clubs.

In the two centuries since his death, a worldwide cult has developed around the poet. Though there may be greater poets, none have surpassed Burns in touching the spirit that bonds people of all nations,

creeds, and colors. For Scots, he is among a handful of writers who popularized the character of the native Scots language. Burns Suppers have taken on a universal meaning. The proceedings for the night may be formal or informal. A formal supper organized by a Burns Club begins when all the guests are seated. A piper enters the room, followed by the cook carrying in the ten- or twenty-pound haggis. Behind him comes the waiter with a bottle of whisky. The procession then walks around the company, ending up at the chairman of the club, who takes the whisky from the waiter and pours out two glasses. The piper stops playing, the haggis is placed on the table, and the piper and the chef are given the whisky. Someone recites Burns's "Address to a Haggis" and before the meal begins someone will recite Burns's famous grace:

> Some hae meat, and canna eat,
> And some wad eat, that want it,
> But we hae meat and we can eat,
> And sae the Lord be thankit.

The menu for the meal might also include a Scotch broth or cock-a-leekie soup, fresh fish, roasted meat, or poultry, and sweet desserts and puddings. The toasting and drinking goes on through the night, accompanied by the singing of Scottish folk songs and recitals of Scottish poetry. The ending is a communal singing of "Auld Lang Syne" when everyone joins hands in a circle.

85

Colcannon

Colcannon is a dish found in the Western Islands of Scotland and also in Ireland. It is made from boiled cabbage, carrots, turnips, and potatoes. This mixture is then drained and stewed for about twenty minutes in a pan with some butter, seasoned with salt and pepper, and served hot.

Perhaps a relative of colcannon, clapshot is delicious with haggis. A traditional Orkney dish, it is widely eaten in the north of Scotland. Potatoes, turnips, shallots, and nutmeg are stewed and then mashed for this dish.

86

Crowdie and Other Cheeses

Relatively little is known about cheesemaking in Scotland before the eleventh century. Cheesemaking relies on a stable pastoral environment, and would have had little place during the warring periods of the Picts and the early Celts. The Vikings, by imposing their culture in northern and western Scotland for over five hundred years, provided a period of comparative stability. Their skills were concentrated in the mining and metalworking crafts, together with cattle raising and fishing, and cheesemaking may have played only a small part in their culture. Over time, however, cheesemaking skills extended into the Western Isles and Hebrides.

It is certain that with the incursion of the Celtic tribes from Ireland and the spread of Christianity in southwestern Scotland, cheesemaking would also have been carried out by monasteries, albeit on a relatively small scale. The role that the Church had in farming and food produc-

tion has long been underestimated, lasting as it did for the best part of one thousand years in Britain. As self-contained communities farmed large areas of land, they kept large flocks of cattle and sheep. Their products, including cheese, would be used by the community and sold where possible as a means of revenue.

The first step toward increasing the role of cheese at a national level came when Kenneth I united the Scots and the Picts and formed a kingdom in central Scotland. This eventually expanded to include Strathclyde and Lothian, the latter originally a part of Northumbria. Malcolm III and his wife (who later became Saint Margaret) continued the development of what was to become a feudal state, which was firmly established when David I became king. He had been brought up in England for many years, and as an "English Scotsman," he was interested in trying to harmonize the workings of the two nations politically and economically. Having retained the ownership of extensive estates in Herefordshire, he arranged for large herds of Highland cattle to be driven down, fattened up on his estates, and then sold in the London market. This was in fact a precursor of a much larger trade in cattle-driving from the western Highlands to England. Having centralized the seat of government in the Forfar area and later Stirling, King David provided the opportunity for accurate records to be kept of what went on in his kingdom, and it is from these records that we know about cheesemaking.

Scotland has only a small number of indigenous cheeses. It was thought that the harsh climate and rugged terrain was not good for cheesemaking, but there were some soft cheeses made by the tenant farmers. Crowdie, the traditional soft cheese of Scotland, is thought to have been introduced by Vikings, although there is no record of it by name until the eighteenth century, possibly because it was usually made only for home consumption. The seasoned whey is squeezed in a muslin bag to remove excess water, left aside for two days, and then rolled in oats and served. Caboc, another traditional Scottish soft cheese, can be traced back to the fifteenth century. Made from double cream and then covered in oatmeal, it has a buttery taste. Dunlop, the only indigenous hard cheese, was first made in the time of James II by Barbara Gilmour, the most influential figure in Scottish cheese history. She learned how to make cheese in Ireland, where she was driven at the time of the religious troubles. On her return to Scotland around 1688, she started making a sweet, milky cheese that was named after the village where she lived. The making of dunlop went on to become a flourishing industry in the eighteenth and nineteenth centuries.

The climate and geography of Scotland are actually well suited to cheesemaking. It was making cheese for export that was difficult. The short cheesemaking season in Scotland meant that traditional cheeses usually required storage through the winter, transportation was difficult, and there was not much money in it. In the last fifteen years, there

has been a renewal in the Scottish cheese industry. Today there are dozens of cheesemakers across Scotland, ranging from large industrial cheddar creameries to several artisan and farmhouse cheesemakers. Scottish cheddar accounts for 70 to 80 percent of the total cheese output. The main creameries are located at Locherbie, Stranraer, Galloway, Loch Arthur, and Campbeltown, and on the islands of Bute, Arran, Islay, Mull, and Orkney (Grimbister).

Lanark blue cheese, with its dark blue veining is often referred to as "The Scottish Roquefort." Dunsyre blu, like Lanark, is a creamy blue cheese with green veining and is quite sharp. Inverloch is a goat cheese made on the island of Gigha. Bonnett, from Ayrshire, is a hard goat cheese. Crowdie now comes in many versions. Gruth Dhu is cream rolled in peppercorns and oatmeal. Hramsa is made with wild garlic leaf and cream. Galic has a covering of chopped toasted hazelnuts.

Of course, since we are talking about Scotland, many of the local cheeses include whisky as an ingredient. Bishop Kennedy is superb soft, creamy cheese that's washed in malt whisky. As it matures, it develops to a pungent, strong cheese. Glenphilly cheddar is blended with eight-year-old malt whisky. Highland choice is a dunlop cheese blended with Drambuie and almond. Glen Moray is a caerphilly-style cheese washed in Glen Moray whisky.

87

Fish

Arbroath smokies are small haddocks, cleaned, salted, and then hung in twos by the tails on wood spits over a fire. This method was developed by Scottish fisherman who settled at Arbroath. These are made inside smokies, fish houses, or sheds. These are not easily available outside Scotland but these fish, having been through a long smoking process, do not need more than a gentle steaming or short baking.

Herrings are served many ways in Scotland. Salted and smoked they are called "red" herrings, for many centuries the staple diet of poor people. They were soaked overnight then boiled on top of potatoes. Gradually, the amount of salt used was reduced to suit public taste. When herrings are cured closed up they are called bloaters, and when they are split open before curing they are called kippers. Herring can be grilled, fried, or cooked in boiling water. It can also be served as an appetizer, and with eggs for breakfast—quite a versatile little fish!

Herring fishing was once one of Scotland's strongest industries. At its peak as a business around 1910, two million barrels were sold a year. Herring also featured prominently in Scottish poems and folk songs and they even inspired the novel *The Silver Darlings* by Neil Gunn.

The rivers Spey, Tay, and Tweed are major salmon fisheries. Since Victorian times these and other rivers have hosted wealthy fishing parties on the estates of the aristocracy. Poaching (illegally catching) salmon is an equally traditional activity. In recent times, many major fish farms have been established in the sea lakes on the western coast of Scotland. These are major commercial sources of fish, although the quality is not considered the same as wild river-caught salmon.

Brown tout, haddock, cod, and plaice are all important fish in Scotland. Highland sauce, made from red wine, vinegar, anchovies, onions, horseradish, and nutmeg, is a Scottish specialty.

Of course, we cannot leave out fish and chips. In hundreds of fish-and-chip stands across Scotland, the fish is dropped into hot fat, fried until brown and crispy, and then drained on absorbent paper. Most establishments serve their fish and chips (french fries) together in a newspaper or brown paper wrapping, with wax paper on the inside to keep it from sticking to the pulp and to keep it hot. Some people top off their treat with a big pickled onion or red beetroot, but the best way to eat fish and chips is to sprinkle on some salt and malt vinegar and eat until

your heart's content—preferably while strolling down the street, the same way most Scottish folks do. If you eat the whole bag using only your fingers, then you have truly experienced "fish and chips."

88

Forfar Bridies and Scotch Pies

Forfar bridies are round, crusty pastry pies baked without using a pie tin, made with finely chopped beef and short-crust pastry like a turnover. Tradition calls for mutton or venison, although in modern times beef is almost always used. A variation of the theme may contain onion in addition to the beef. Differentiating between the ordinary pie and the onion variety was traditionally made easier by the number of holes in the top: one for plain, two for onion. Perhaps the best-known maker was Wallace's Pie Shop in Dundee.

The Scotch pie is an oval delicacy made with the filling crimped into the pastry case. The pastry may be either plain or flaky. The plain pastry is made by preparing a stiff paste of flour and water, seasoned with a pinch of salt. It is rolled out into an oval shape about five by seven inches, and minced beef, a little suet, and a sprinkling of very finely chopped onion is placed in the center. The pastry is then folded

over along its longest dimension, brushed with milk, and cooked until golden brown.

Mutton pies were known in Glasgow as "Tuppenyl struggles" and traditionally were made with hot-water pastry, but you can use short-cut pastry as well.

89

Game

Scotland is fortunate to have some of the finest game in the world. And although we don't choose to wolf down heron or swan as our medieval ancestors did, we still have plenty to choose from. From the start of the season (August 12, when the grouse season starts) until February, we can choose from a variety of furred and feathered game.

From the more common pheasant, venison, and partridge to the rarer roe deer, teal, widgeon, and hare, there is a large variety at butchers throughout Scotland. One of the most natural of all foods, game is free from additives or chemical feed. And because game is by nature wild, the animals or birds have to work extremely hard to obtain their food and so have very little fat on them. In these days of low-fat, lean cuisine, game surely constitutes an ideal modern food.

Although game was originally eaten by all (prehistoric man's diet

was not all roots and berries), it gradually became exclusive to the wealthy and remained so until relatively recently. Pictures of great haunches of venison served up on large silver platters surrounded by pomp and ceremony suggest baronial splendor, the fare of landed gentry rather then tenant farmers. But prices have come down in Scotland and game is no longer exclusive.

Because game is so lean, it should be cooked judiciously. As a general rule, either fast roast or slowly braise with plenty of liquid to keep it moist and tender. If you opt for fast roasting at a very high temperature, then do not overcook or it will dry out and become tough. Resting the meat once it is out of the oven relaxes it and ensures even cooking all the way through. For slow-cooking, provided there is plenty of wine or stock, it will be tender but well-cooked. As a general rule, always braise older birds or animals, but if unsure of the age, then take the safe bet and sling it in the casserole for a long, slow stew.

Grouse is associated firmly with the Glorious Twelfth of August (the opening of hunting season), but in fact eating this bird later in the season, when prices come down, is better. Grouse is best served roasted, made in a casserole, or made part of game terrines. Pheasants are perhaps the most versatile of all game as their flavor is milder than most and indeed some is akin in taste to free-range chicken. Venison is less expensive these days since much is farmed, which also means it is avail-

able all year round. Hare and rabbit make excellent pasta sauces and casseroles, and hare in particular makes a truly wonderful Scottish soup called bawd bree, which my father recalls his grandmother cooking for the family on Christmas Day, before turkey made it all the way north to Dundee.

90

Haggis

My mother never made haggis, since just the recipe itself is daunting. One of the original recipes included one cleaned sheep's stomach bag; oatmeal; chopped mutton suet; a pound of lamb or venison (prefered) liver, boiled and minced; and sheep heart, boiled and finely chopped—all flavored with onions, cayenne, salt, pepper, and allspice. The chopped ingredients were stuffed into the sheep's stomach and boiled for three hours. Fortunately, for those who love it, haggis can now be bought in the supermarket in Scotland.

My parents took me to Scotland when I was sixteen, and the first day in Edinburgh my father made me order haggis so that I could "experience" a real Scottish dish. As the famous Boswell once said, "Once was enough."

Haggis is the most traditional of all Scottish dishes, and was ele-

vated to great heights by Scotland's national poet Robert Burns. In his "Address to the Haggis," he wrote:

Fair fa' yer honest, sonsie face,
Great chieftain o' the pudden race!

Haggis is featured on the menu of every dinner honoring the poet, usually held on Burns Night, January 25, his birthday. There are Burns Suppers all over the world and I recently saw one advertised in New York (it was very expensive, I noted). Hogmanay (New Year's Eve) is another time for serving haggis, accompanied by the traditional black bun, het pint, and shortbread. And of course, it must be accompanied by small glasses of neat Scotch whisky. Haggis was always a popular dish at Martinmas. The entrails of the animals that were slaughtered were mixed with oatmeal and stuffed into a sheep's bladder to be boiled. Spices were added to help to preserve them. Another favorite that used up the blood was black puddings. White mealy puddings were also popular.

Perhaps the best-known maker of haggis is the Edinburgh company of Charles MacSween & Son (now relocated out of the city). Their haggis is widely available in the U.K. and they will happily ship it overseas, although note that the strict agriculture regulations preclude importing

haggis into the U.S. MacSweens also makes a vegetarian "haggis," which is actually quite tasty, even though the only ingredient it has in common with the real thing is the oatmeal.

91

Hot Toddies and Other Nice Drinks

To make a hot toddie, place a teaspoon of sugar and a teaspoon of Scottish heather honey in a warm glass. Add a measure of Scotch whisky (preferably not a malt) and top it off with boiling water. The drink is traditionally stirred gently with a silver spoon. This, it is said, will cure anything.

Like the English, Scots love their beer. Scottish brews are usually darker and sweeter than English beer and served in pints and half pints. Real ales are served from the pump, and Scotch ale, known as "heavy," is a favorite. As mentioned earlier, heather ales are a specialty. Strong ales like barley wine have a high alcohol content and are sold as "nips." A traditional aperitif in Scotland is a glass of sherry, and for dessert claret is preferred over port. Drambuie is a golden liqueur, based on Scotch whisky, that is sweetened with heather honey and flavored with different herbs.

92

Malt Whisky

Although blended whiskies dominate the market, most consumers would agree that malts are more fun. There are many single malts and they all have their own distinctive taste. They vary enormously depending on the water, peat, and oak barrels used in the distilling and maturing process.

When the water flows off the mountains down to the distilleries, it often runs through peat, thus adding character to the whisky. The peat is cut and burned to help germinate and malt the barley, which is fermented. The amount of peat smoke used at this stage affects the flavor. Particularly peaty malts are made on the Islands, and the Highlands. There are four distinct malt groups: Highland, Lowland, Islay, and Campbletown, with the majority falling into the Highland category and produced largely alongside the Spey River.

Islay is the island whisky capital of the world. Here, off the western

coast, not far from Northern Ireland, there are currently seven working distilleries; Ardbeg, (recently reopened), Bowmore, Bunnahabhain, Bruichladdich, Caol Ila, Lagavulin, and Laphroaig. Port Ellen distilled up to 1983, although it still produces malt for the others. Islay malts are distinctively peaty and smoky, but each has its own characteristics.

The long island of Jura, whose name means in Norse "island of the deer," is home to a distillery that can trace its roots back to the seventeenth century. The dark peaty water for the stills falls from a lake for over one thousand feet to the distillery in the island's only village. It is a surprisingly light color and not as peaty as an Islay malt, but you can detect traces of seaside saltiness after the initial sweetness.

Glenkinchie, from the great barley-producing area of East Lothian, is the most widely available single malt from the Lowlands. It is light-straw colored and sweetish, with a fine floral nose.

93

Marmalade

Marmalade is a food that has become associated with Scotland. It is made of a citrus fruit—usually oranges—cooked with sugar, and possibly other ingredients, to form a set jelly. Nowadays it is served on bread or toast, or incorporated into desserts.

The Romans discovered the process of making jelly by heating and then cooling a combination of fruit, acid, and sugars, the same method used in all modern jams and marmalades. They traditionally preserved fruits in honey, but they found that quinces weren't suitable for being preserved in this way, so they precooked the quinces in wine before adding the honey. This caused pectin to be released and the mixture set to form a quince jelly. The Romans used this jelly as a medicine for indigestion and poor appetite.

In Anglo-Saxon times, rosehips (and possibly other fruits) were preserved by being boiled down, with or without honey added, and

stored in jars. The Anglo-Saxons served meats with a variety of fruit sauces. Oranges and lemons were first shipped to the U.K. from Spain in the thirteenth century, either as whole fruit, or as fruit and peel preserved in sugar syrup. Oranges were still used for medicinal purposes, and were believed to promote "good appetite." In the fifteenth century, quince "marmelada" was imported from Portugal. By 1495, it was arriving in sufficient quantities to be assessed for duty by customs officials. Marmelada was quite solid, so it was cut with a knife and served in slices as part of the final course of a feast. It was flavored with rosewater and either musk or ambergris. One popular marmalade in Scotland was "orange chip,"made using extra pieces of orange peel.

In 1608, the aphrodisiac properties of marmalades were being discussed. Queen Mary Tudor used a marmalade made of quinces, orange peel, sugar, almonds, rosewater, musk, ambergris, cinamon, cloves, ginger, and mace to help her get pregnant. (It didn't work.) Mary Queen of Scots is reputed to have used orange marmalade (sent from her childhood home in France) as a medicine. In the 1640s, sugar from Barbados was becoming more widely available and it began to be used in more fruit conserves and other desserts. In the late seventeenth and eighteenth centuries "marmalade madam" was a name for a prostitute.

Dundee is the home of bitter orange marmalade. Dundee marmalade was introduced to the commercial market by the firm of James Keiller of Dundee at the beginning of the nineteenth century. According

to Keiller family legend, James Keiller bought a cargo of Seville oranges very cheaply from a Spanish ship sheltering from a storm in Dundee harbor. He then found that they were so bitter that no one would buy them as eating fruit. The story says that his wife Janet made them into a jam, creating the famous "bitter" marmalade. What the Keiller family did was take orange chip marmalade, add more visible peel, and market the marmalade as an aid to breakfast digestion. When John Mitchell Keiller entered the family firm, he ensured the company's firm control over the production of marmalade by registering Keiller's Dundee Orange Marmalade as one of the first trademarks, following new trademark legislation in 1876. He eventually took over the company.

By the 1870s, Dundee Marmalade was being bought in Australia, New Zealand, South Africa, India, and China—mainly to British expatriate consumers. By the end of last century, its fame was global. Keillers did not invent marmalade, but what they did was to make one particular version—orange chip marmalade, increasingly favored by domestic jam makers in Scotland—improved, standardized, and promoted. That is how they made their fortune.

94

Neeps 'n' Tatties and Rumbledthumps

Neeps 'n' tatties is the classic accompaniment to haggis, and is remarkably simple to make. Just peel, chop, and boil roughly equal quantities of potato and turnip or swede, and then drain and mash them together with a little butter and seasoning. Make sure you don't forget the haggis.

Rumbledthumps are a variation, made by frying some cabbage (preferably kale) in a little oil and mixing in mashed potatoes. For an interesting variation, add some chopped chives to the potatoes before mashing them.

95

Oats

"Oats: a grain which in England is generally given to a horse, but in Scotland it supports the people." In spite of Samuel Johnson's witty and caustic remark, oats are popular all over the world. Americans consume it in the form of cooked oatmeal, dry oatmeal cereals, oatmeal cookies, and muffins.

Classic Scottish porridge is made by boiling half a pint of water, then slowly stirring in one ounce of oatmeal. It needs to be simmered gently for about twenty-five minutes and stirred continuously with the traditional *spirtle*—a wooden stick about twelve inches long—to avoid any lumps. A little salt can be added halfway through. The porridge is then left to stand for two minutes before eating. Porridge should be thick and wholesome, not thin like gruel. Traditionally porridge is served in one bowl, with cold milk in another. Each spoonful of porridge is dipped into the milk before it is eaten—but on no account

should any sugar be added. Porridge must be cooked with salt to obtain the correct flavor. Those eating porridge outside Scotland have been known to cook it without salt and indeed eat it with sugar or even syrup, a habit that would turn the stomach of any Scotsman (or Scotswoman).

Traditionally, workers in the Highlands would make a large pot of porridge at the beginning of the week. Once allowed to cool, it would be cut into slices, and a man would put a slice in his pocket each day for lunch. Today it is often eaten for breakfast, with the addition of milk, and a small plate keeps you feeling full until lunchtime.

Oats are used in many other Scottish specialties. Broonie is a traditional Orkney oatmeal gingerbread. The name comes from the Norse *bruni,* meaning a thick bannock. Skirlie, also called mealie pudding, is made with oatmeal, onions, and suet (or pan drippings). It is a side dish for meats and fish and is also used to stuff chicken and lamb.

96

Scotch Whisky

The Gaelic expression *uisge beatha* (pronounced oos-kay-ba) means "water of life," and the word "whisky" is derived from it. The word can be traced as far back as the mid-thirteenth century in Ireland, and in his first English dictionary Dr. Johnson used it to describe "a compound distilled spirit, being drawn on aromatics . . . in Scottish they call it whisky."

Initially, whisky was lauded for its medicinal qualities and prescribed for the preservation of health, the prolongation of life, and for the relief of colic, palsy, smallpox, and a host of other ailments. The Scots used whisky from the cradle right up to their life's end. It became an intrinsic part of Scottish life—a reviver and stimulant during the long, cold winters, and a feature of social life, a welcome offering to guests upon arrival at their destinations.

Smart distillers such as Tommy Dewar and John Walker realized

that their English neighbors, not to mention the Americans, didn't much like the traditional Scottish malts. They responded by making whisky "smoother and more appealing to the Southern palate." In 1831, Aeneas Coffey invented the Coffey or patent still, which enabled a continuous process of distillation to take place. This led to the production of grain whisky, a different, less intense spirit than the malt whisky produced in the distinctive copper pot stills. This invention was first exploited by Andrew Usher & Co. who, in 1860, blended malt and grain whisky together for the first time to produce a lighter flavored whisky—extending the appeal of Scotch whisky to a wider market. A law passed by the British Parliament in 1915 prohibits the sale of any distillation of less than three years as Scotch whisky. To comply with the law, it has to be aged in oak wood, usually previously used for bourbon or sherry, in a warehouse controled by the Ministry of Customs and Excise. Whisky improves as it matures in years, and good malt is best between ten and twenty years.

Scotch whisky, like malt whisky, is produced in four areas: Lowland, Island, Campbletown, and Highland, of which the latter is by far the largest. The shores of the Spey River are part of the Highlands but deserve a category of their own. Highland whisky varies enormously from Pulteney of Wick to Tullybardine in the south of Perthshire, Glenury Royal in Kincardine on the eastern coast, and Ben Nevis in the far west.

It is impossible to categorize them in flavor bouquet or body, as they are so diverse.

Although only one whisky is allowed to call itself "The Glenlivet," this bleak Banffshire glen stretches for over fourteen miles, and in its wide breadth there are many distilleries. Two hundred years ago there were well over two hundred of them producing illegally, and the quality of the water flowing off the granite of the mountains, and through peat, has much to do with their fame. Teachers, one of the world's most famous blends, was developed by a Glasgow grocer, William Teacher. His blend was one of the reasons his business expanded to eighteen shops by the 1850s, and today over two million cases a year are shipped bearing his name. Largely Highland and Speyside in character, it is known for its creaminess and its well-rounded smoothness.

I could go on and on about Scotch, since it has always been my drink of choice (as a young woman, I preferred Johnny Walker Red Label to Black Label), but whichever kind you choose is a matter of personal taste.

97

Shortbread

Perhaps it's not surprising that a product as excellent as Walkers Shortbread should have come out of Scotland. After all, the Scots are renowned for their inventiveness and ingenuity! Though it's now a year-round favorite, this tender-crisp, butter-rich cookie was once associated mainly with Christmas and Hogmanay. The traditional round shape comes from the ancient Yule bannock, which was notched around the edges to signify the sun's rays. The classic way of making shortbread is to press the dough into a shallow earthenware mold that is decoratively carved. After baking, the large round cookie is turned out of the mold and cut into wedges. Caramel shortcake is often called "millionaires' shortbread"—presumably because it is so rich.

98

Smoked Salmon

Tweed kettle or salmon hash, made with fresh salmon, is an Edinburgh special. No one knows when our coastal ancestors first noticed that some foods washed in the sea kept longer than foods washed in fresh water. When the first accidental discovery of the preserved—and edible—effects of a dead animal lying upon a naturally occurring lake salt bed took place remains a mystery.

The preserving and curing processes employed by our ancestors in prehistory, were just that—a method of storing produce before the days of refrigeration, using salt as the preserving agent. Space for storage of the salted products then became imperative and most of this food would have been kept in underground chambers or caches. When these were full, the roof spaces in occupied huts and caves were used with varying degrees of success, as these areas were not as cool as the chambers. In an age before chimneys, smoke from the cooking fires would

have collected in certain areas in the roof spaces where some salted fish or meat was stored. Again, we don't know who first realized that, kept in the places where the smoke gathered, the fish and meat remained edible for longer and (dare we say) had a better flavor.

Although the use of salt and smoke to cure and preserve is part of our ancestors' ancient history, the scientific reasons why this should happen are relatively newly discovered. For thousands of years, salting and smoking foods took place for the purpose of preservation and long-term storage. These foods were very salty, and many required soaking in fresh water to remove salt before they were edible, or were so strongly flavored with smoke as to make them almost inedible or at the very least an "acquired" taste.

Smoked salmon is available everywhere, but its quality varies greatly. You will sometimes see "Scottish smoked salmon" at specialty stores at prices much higher than other smoked salmon.

99

Soor Plooms and Other Candies and Desserts

Scots have a collective sweet tooth, a very sweet tooth! Our buns, doughnuts, and cakes, if not covered in a liberal sprinkling of powdered sugar, will be, more often than not, covered in a veneer of sugar icing. We love our fudge, boilings (boiled sweets), such as rhubarb rock and soor plooms, not to mention sweet drinks. Our "other" national drink is irn bru—it is orange and sweet, and Scotland is one of the very few countries where Coca Cola is *not* the number-one selling brand of soft drink! Irn bru is.

Cranachan was the traditional celebration, harvest-home dish. For a communal celebration round the table, the oatmeal, fruit, and cream were put onto the table and everyone made his or her own mix, lubricating it with whisky and honey. Cranachan is a popular Scottish dessert

and there are many variations and names such as cream crowdie, eaten on other special occasions such as weddings. Scotch trifle is made from custard, sponge cakes, jam, and sherry (and/or whisky or brandy), and topped with sweetened cream and garnished with slivered almonds.

Butterscotch is made with brown sugar, creamed butter, and lemon or ginger. A traditional Scots toffee can be flavored with cinnamon, clove, ginger, lemon, orange, peppermint, vanilla, or nuts. Petticoat tails—crisp little biscuitlike cakes—were said to be a favorite of Mary Queen of Scots.

The Scots' love of candy shows up in both dental and heart problems, but this does not stop Scots "soukin awa" on all types of sweeties. The border towns are particularly famous for having their own local brand of sweets: Hawick for Hawick balls; Jedburgh for Jeddart snails; Peebles and Galashiels for soor plooms; and Moffat for Moffat toffee. Melrose, in the past, gave us Coltart's Candy.

Brightly colored Edinburgh rock candy is a traditional favorite and fun to make with children on a rainy day. The following flavors are popular (use a few drops of whichever you select): raspberry, vanilla, orange, peppermint, lemon, and ginger. You can also cheat with a little food coloring to brighten the color, but only in addition to the flavors.

100

Soups

Scotch broth (also known as Scots broth or hotch-potch) is a rich stock, traditionally made by boiling mutton (the neck is best), beef, marrow bone, or chicken (for a chicken broth). It is filled with a choice of root vegetables, which should be diced. Carrots, leeks, cabbage, turnips, and a stick of celery can all be used. The hard vegetables should be added first to the boiling stock, with a handful of barley, and softer vegetables like garden peas added later. The final consistency should be thick and served piping hot. It was not a favorite of English writer Johnson. "You never ate it before?" he was once asked, according to Boswell's *Life of Johnson*. "No sire," replied Johnson, "but I don't care how soon I eat it again."

Cullen skink is made with smoked haddock and potatoes, and partan bree is a soup made with crab and ride. Poacher's soup includes whatever game is available. Mary Queen of Scots's favorite soup was cock-a-

leekie (boiled chicken with leeks), which is actually more of a stew than a soup. When it includes cooked prunes is it called cock-a-leekie à la Talleyrand (a favorite of French statesman Talleyrand).

Powsowdie, a soup made with sheep's head, barley, and dried peas, would be another soup that Johnson probably would not have liked.

101

Stovies

In the past when money and food were in short supply, Scots knew how to make the most of their meager resources. Stovies are a good example of a peasant dish that combined any leftover meat with plenty of potatoes, the mainstay of the tenant farmer's diet in the nineteenth century. Being mainly potato, it provided energy in the form of starch and had enough bulk to fill empty stomachs. Despite the dish's "poor"origins it is very tasty, filling, and often served with oatcakes at *ceilidhs* (country dances) and evening wedding receptions.

Stovies should be made by frying onion in beef drippings in a large pot. Scraps of meat and leftover vegetables are added. Next comes some water and then the potatoes, peeled and thinly sliced. Salt is added and the pot is left to simmer until the potatoes are soft, adding only a little water as needed.

Conclusion

No, we Scots are not perfect, but pretty nearly so. An old Scottish proverb says, "Wink at small faults, for you have great ones yourself." We have a rich if tumultuous history, and have made some astonishing contributions to the world.

Here's something the Scots can be truly proud of: The Homelessness (Scotland) Act, passed in 2003 by the Scottish parliament in Edinburgh, is intended to ensure that by 2012 every unintentionally homeless person will be entitled to permanent accommodation. The act, which received cross-party support and was widely welcomed by homelessness charities, is the most progressive homelessness legislation in Western Europe. As well as guaranteeing a home to all Scots, it offers greater legal protection to those who are homeless or who are in danger of becoming homeless by changing the process of repossession, one of the key causes of homelessness. For people who are judged to have made themselves intentionally homeless, there will be new support in the form of probationary tenancies, which will allow them to get back into society.